TRYIN' TO GET TO YOU

The Story of Elvis Presley

by VALERIE HARMS

AN AUTHORS GUILD BACKINPRINT.COM EDITION

Tryin' to Get to You:
The Story of Elvis Presley
All Rights Reserved © 1979, 2000 by Valerie Harms

No part of this book may be reproduced or transmitted in any form
or by any means, graphic, electronic, or mechanical, including photocopying,
recording, taping, or by any information storage or retrieval system,
without the permission in writing from the publisher.

AN AUTHORS GUILD BACKINPRINT.COM EDITION

Published by iUniverse.com, Inc.

For information address:
iUniverse.com, Inc.
620 North 48th Street, Suite 201
Lincoln, NE 68504-3467
www.iuniverse.com

Originally published by Atheneum/SMI

Photo and lyric credits are on page 177.

ISBN: 0-595-09298-5

Printed in the United States of America

Tryin' to Get to You
The Story of Elvis Presley

Contents

1: Elvis Is Born   3
2: Roots in Mississippi   9
3: The Contest   16
4: First Guitar   22
5: Memphis   28
6: Kickoff   33
7: Present for Mama   39
8: Gettin' It Together at Sun Records   47
9: Starting Down the Road   55
10: The Pivotal Point   64
11: Elvis Is Pressed — at Sun Records and Elsewhere   74
12: Big Business   84
13: Television   93
14: Movies   100
15: Land of Grace   108
16: The Crunch   115
17: Germany   123
18: Disillusioned Movie Actor   130
19: Marriage and Other Changes   139
20: Comeback   149
21: Elvis Plays the King   159
22: Decline   168

Tryin' to Get to You
The Story of Elvis Presley

1: Elvis Is Born

Vernon Presley stood by the window and nervously watched his wife, Gladys, breathe deeply and groan as she lay on their rumpled bed, trying to push the baby out of her body. He'd never seen a baby come before, and he was too nervous to go up close. The doctor wiped perspiration from Gladys's white face. Vernon shivered even though he had a sweater on under his old jacket. What a cold day to be born — January 8, 1935. Rags had been stuffed in the windows to keep the cold air out.

"Go get me some water. We're going to need it soon," said the doctor. Vernon was glad to do something useful. On his way outside to the water pump, he passed through the kitchen — the house's only other room — where his and Gladys's sisters and brothers sat crowded around the table and waited for news.

"Have some hot beans and coffee," one said. Vernon shook his head. He was in no mood to eat. They resumed their talk. "I don't know, but if Franklin Roosevelt isn't the President who can turn this country around, I don't know who can."

The two-room home in Tupelo, Mississippi, where Elvis was born

"I don't think he can bring us back our cotton mill." (Vernon knew his brother, Vester, complained because he'd just lost his job at the mill.)

"No one's hirin' because nothin's comin' in good this year. Nothin' planted, nothin' harvested. Hard times all around."

"Amen."

Vernon trotted down the steps of the porch of the house he built with his brother's help. The earth was so rocky and worn out that he knew it couldn't grow any vegetables. They didn't have any money and he was worried about what his family was going to do. Everyone in Tupelo, Mississippi, was suffering.

Elvis Is Born   5

He primed the pump until the water started to flow into his bucket. Nearby was the toilet shack; it didn't smell so bad in the wintry air. Vernon gave the water pump a kick. Here he was, only eighteen years old, with a wife and a baby coming, and the only work he could find was driving a milk truck. Shoot, that wouldn't earn him enough to keep the baby alive.

When he reentered the kitchen, he heard a long scream come from Gladys that chilled him to the bone. Everyone stopped talking. Vernon rushed to the front room. The doctor triumphantly held aloft a small, scrunched-up baby. "It's a boy. Right fine one too. Get that water heated up now."

His sister took the bucket from his hand, as he went over to watch. The baby was no bigger than one of his shoes. His eyes were closed and his mouth no wider than a button. His legs and arms fanned the air as if unsure of his balance in such wide open space. He had thin dark hair. Vernon ran his fingers in amazement through his own wavy blond hair. He was afraid to reach out and touch the fragile baby.

"Let me have him," said Gladys. The doctor laid the baby on Gladys's breast and went to see about the bath water. Vernon sat down on the bed and put his arm around Gladys. He had never seen her look so exhausted. Her black hair straggled damply across the pillow. She held the baby with weak hands. Smiling at Vernon she said, "Well here is Elvis Aron." Vernon leaned down and gave her a kiss.

Then they laughed because suddenly the whole family surrounded the bed, each one wanting to be the one to pick him up and bathe him. Finally, Faye, Gladys's best friend, washed him while the doctor held his squirming body and kept his head above water. Elvis cried loudly until long after he was wrapped in a towel and cuddled by Faye.

"Doctor," Gladys said, "I still feel pain. I think there's another baby in me!"

The doctor felt her uterus. "Sure enough. It's not in the right position though. And you're losing a lot of blood. I wish we were in a hospital now." Fear went through Vernon. If only they could afford the hospital! Women could die in childbirth.

Gladys sighed. Her body stiffened, then shuddered. The relatives became quiet and fixed their eyes on her, waiting. Even a hush came over Elvis, as the doctor worked over Gladys, assisting in her struggle.

Gladys was right. There was another baby. A boy. Only he was born dead. He would have been Elvis's twin. "Oh," Gladys cried, "we'd have named him Jesse."

Tears rolled from her eyes to the pillow, as she mourned losing the baby she'd carried so long inside her. Vernon held her hand and with the other arm squeezed the tiny Elvis to his chest. Somehow he had the feeling that this infant was the only one he'd be lucky enough to get, and he was sure going to take care of him.

Vernon's father left to make a wooden box for the dead baby's burial.

Gladys' mother, Minnie said, "Elvis will always miss his twin. He'll be like the missing piece in a jigsaw puzzle."

Night came. The doctor had long since gone. So had the relatives, after leaving some warm food on the stove. The coffin was sealed and placed in a corner of the front room until the morning.

A fire blazed in the hearth, sending out the only warmth and light in the room. Shadows flickered on the walls where the paint peeled off. Vernon sat in a straight chair turned toward the fire, tired and anxious about Gladys. She had been working as a sewing machine operator, but now she would need time to get well again and take care of the baby.

In bed Gladys, dressed in a clean flannel gown, dozed and awoke with a start. Her husband looked handsome, she reflected. Next to her in the crook of her arm lay baby Elvis, sleeping peacefully. She pulled the blankets over his chest and watched him tenderly. Her own body felt calm at last. She listened to Elvis breathe and, closing her eyes, thanked the Lord for delivering them through the day.

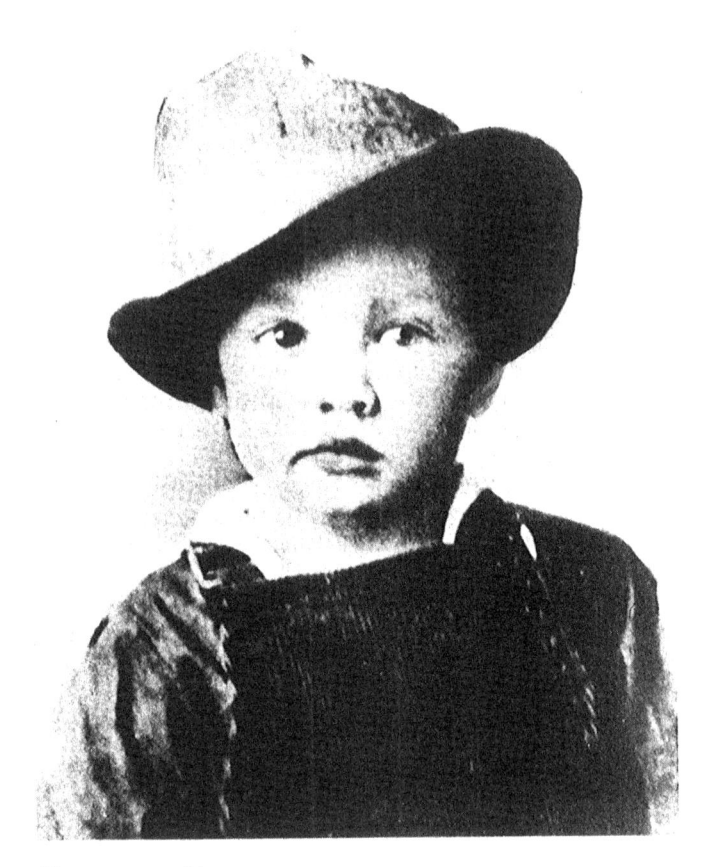

Two years old

2: Roots in Mississippi

Six-year-old Elvis, dressed in hand-me-down overalls that were too short for him, ran out of his house onto the dirt road in front. "Elvis, come here this minute," called his mother from inside. "Don't you run away now." Elvis squatted in the road to make sure that the fort he'd built with stones was still there. Although he'd just had a breakfast of milk and corn bread, he was hungry. He laughed at an ant carrying a big fly.

Vernon and Gladys came out and shut the rickety door. This house was even shabbier than their former one, which they hadn't been able to afford any more. Here there were holes in the walls and broken windows. Vernon was learning how to be a carpenter so he could get a steady job but it was not easy.

"Come on, Elvis," Vernon said. Gladys took him by the hand and the three set off down the road together. As a baby Elvis was carried to the First Assembly of God Church, now he walked. The family always wore their Sunday best: for Vernon that meant an old jacket over washed

Elvis, in hand-me-down clothes, with his mother, Gladys, and father Vernon.

but stained pants, for Gladys a tan dress and brown pumps.

They waved to Mrs. Grimes, the widowed teacher, who lived in a house like theirs just down the road. She was hanging out a big sheet to dry.

Farther on they came to the black neighborhood called "Shakerag," saying "howdy" to folks sitting on their porches in the Sunday morning sun. Elvis watched kids playing in a circle, chanting "Tisket a tasket, green and yellow basket/sent a letter to my love/and on the way I dropped it." A boy dropped a pebble behind a girl who took off madly chasing him. Elvis wanted to play with them.

"We cain't be late," said his mother, tugging his hand as he took one last look.

At the fish hatchery Elvis let go of her hand and ran ahead to the big pond. The surface of the pond was covered with lily pads and bugs zipping back and forth. Below were supposed to be thousands of fish, which Elvis strained to see but couldn't. A frog croaked near the edge. Elvis made a face and croaked back at it. All around the pond were big shade trees. "Let's stay here," he said as Vernon scooped him up in his arms.

"Maybe later." Vernon carried him over the railroad tracks and then set him down again. They passed the garment factory and old cotton mill, talking casually.

In town the houses were closer together. The church looked like just another house except it had a peaked roof and was freshly painted white. As they neared the steps Vernon and Gladys greeted some of their sisters' and brothers' families. They all went in together, just like they did every Wednesday for the revival meetings.

Elvis's cousin George had something hidden in his hand. Elvis said, "Watcha got?" George showed him a pack of bubble gum. Elvis's eyes widened, but George slipped it into his back pocket. Elvis was placed between his mother and father on the pew so that he and George couldn't talk to each other.

On the raised altar the chorus of men and women sang "How Sweet Thy Spirit" in low voices. Elvis watched his uncle, who had a deep bass voice. His uncle had taught him some of the songs and so when Elvis recognized a tune, he sang along with them or else he hummed.

The preacher, tall and thin, stood up in his black suit and led the congregation in a prayer. He began talking to the congregation in a calm, serious way about "war." Elvis was afraid as he listened to the preacher speak louder and more intensely. "In Mississippi, we've just made our peace with the Indians . . . Bad enough when we are at war with our own native Americans. Then came World War I. You'd think we learned a lesson about killing. No, now we are embroiled in another world war. Many of our families have lost their lives." Elvis looked at his daddy's grim face. He didn't want his daddy to be a soldier and die. His mama looked worried too. "Let us call on God to be with us," the preacher concluded.

The congregation stood and sang "The Lord's

Prayer," which was so beautiful to sing that Elvis began to feel better.

The preacher came down off the platform, talking about "calling on God to take away our sins. We have sinned too much. Let us become clean." He shook hands with those near the aisles. "Let's make a joyful noise unto the Lord," he urged them. The group sang again, this time louder and more fervently. "Singing is praying," the preacher shouted. He moved back to the platform altar, chanting to God, praying and singing with the others. His body began to shake. So did the others.

"Halleleuia," he thundered and the people thundered the word back. They all stood and sang in their strongest voices. Elvis too.

"You got the spirit!" his grandmother, Minnie, said to him from behind. Elvis loved the power in the swelling sounds. It was thrilling to join his small voice to it. The pianist pounded the keys, his body bent and rocking, just like the preacher's body as it danced across the platform, touching those who came up to him, helping them with their problems.

People called out, "Amen," "Oh Jesus," "Make me clean," as the furor reached an ecstatic pitch. Elvis felt electrified. It was the music and the singing that shook his bones beneath his skin and seemed to carry him up to the sky. Oh yes, God was with them, right there in the songs.

Gladys bent down and hugged Elvis fiercely. She looked radiant.

"Praise God," said the preacher softly. "Let us thank God." The chorus sang a light, joyful song. It calmed the congregation like a steady summer rain.

Afterwards the families filed out, and while they talked among themselves in front of the Church, Elvis chased George across the lawn to ask for a piece of the bubble gum but George kept dodging around bushes. Finally he fell down giggling and rolled in the grass.

"Honey, you pick yourself up this minute," called Gladys. "We're going to Uncle Vester's." His uncle and aunt and cousins started walking away, while his mother and father waited for him to catch up.

They walked out of town onto another dirt road until they came to an old farmhouse. The grownups went inside and the four children sat down on the porch steps looking for something to do. There were no toys or bicycles or balls. And it was too crowded to play inside. Elvis found an old Coke bottle and blew across the top to make it hum. The others tried filling it up with water and then blowing. That didn't sound so good. One of the boys squirted the water at his sister. She chased him into a ditch across the road.

"Y'all come eat now," hollered his aunt.

The kids straggled in, one by one, getting their hands and faces wiped off by Gladys. Vernon and Vester already sat at the kitchen table, which was set with steaming bowls of pea soup with chunks of ham and mashed potatoes and corn on the cob.

The families sat down eagerly. It was their biggest meal of the week, their only meat, and they were hungry.

3: The Contest

Elvis sang at school too. Every day his fifth-grade teacher, the same Mrs. Grimes who'd been his neighbor (the Presley's house had been condemned so they'd moved again to another poor section of Tupelo), began the morning with a prayer and a hymn. She asked the children to volunteer but when they didn't, she took turns calling on them.

Elvis dreaded his turn, but when he was called upon he stood by his desk and blurted, "Ma'am, I know a song about a dog who goes to heaven." Chuckles came from the twenty-five other boys and girls.

White-haired, sharp-nosed Mrs. Grimes tapped her knuckles on the desk. "All right, that will do. Go ahead."

Elvis fidgeted with the threads worn loose on his shirt cuff. Shyly he began to sing about Old Shep, a dog who was so faithful he saved a boy from drowning. When Elvis got to the part where the doctor said Old Shep had to be killed, his voice wavered and he had to take a deep breath. At the end he sat down quickly.

Mrs. Grimes said, "Very nice. Not quite right

The Contest   17

for morning chapel but it'll do, it'll do." She wiped her eyes.

Elvis was glad Mrs. Grimes liked the song, for later that day she gave him a Coke to sing it for Mr. Andrews, the grocery store owner.

The next week she asked him to sing it again at school, this time when the principal, Mr. Cole, visited their class. After he heard the song, Mr. Cole said, "Elvis, I'd like to see you in my office before you go home."

"Yes, sir," Elvis mumbled, afraid he'd gotten himself into trouble.

Later in Mr. Cole's office, the plump, bald-headed man said, "Lad, that was a pretty nice song this morning. Where'd you learn how to sing?"

"Church, sir." Elvis looked down at his scuffed shoes.

"This weekend is the Mississippi-Alabama Fair, where there's a singing contest. I think you're good enough to enter."

Elvis looked at him, stunned. "I'm — I mean — I'm not good enough."

"Would you like to try?"

Elvis froze. He was glad Mr. Cole liked his singing, but was terrified of singing in front of a bunch of people! "I don't know."

"Well, I'm going on Saturday. Tell your folks I'll drive you — and them too, if you're willing."

"Yes, sir."

When Elvis's mother met him at school to walk him home, he told her all about Mr. Cole's offer. She looked as surprised as he was but then she put her arm around his thin shoulders and said, "You are my precious baby." In almost no time she had alerted his grandparents, aunts, uncles, and cousins. They were all sure to be at the Fair. Elvis would have liked to have died.

The country fair was the year's biggest event. It was always held at harvest time so the farmers could show off their best crops. They prepared months in advance to bring their best chickens, cattle, pigs, and sheep; others brought preserves and pies for sale.

Saturday morning Gladys boiled some water and put Elvis in the tub and scrubbed his hair and neck herself. "Oh Mama," he complained, "I don't see why all the fuss." Her rubbing and tugging made his stomach ache.

"You gotta look good when all those people watch you." She giggled. "I just cain't believe my little boy is going to sing at the Fair!" More than ever Elvis wished he didn't have to.

"I think the boy's too young myself," said Vernon. He was annoyed because he had only a dollar in his pocket to spend and he didn't want to be embarrassed.

But when Mr. Cole honked for them, the three were all excited to set forth under the clear blue sky. While Mr. Cole and his parents chatted, Elvis sat with his face pressed against the window, aware of his heart pounding. He was the first to spot the colored flags flying from the tents and the ferris wheel.

After parking the car in a big field, they walked to the first tent along with crowds of other people. Elvis watched a parade of horses circling a ring. A gorgeous palomino with flowing white mane and tail came toward him. He was about to tell his daddy that he wished he could ride a horse like that someday but something stopped him.

In another tent a beauty contest was going on. A dozen girls in bathing suits and high heels sat on a platform. One girl with long, fluffy black hair walked in front of a judge's stand. Elvis stared at the girl's perfectly made-up face. Never had he seen anyone so beautiful. "Is she a movie star?" he asked. The girl heard the remark and smiled at him. His parents laughed. Gladys took him by the hand until they came to the singing contest.

On the platform, a man with a banjo in his arm and a harmonica propped on his chest was singing away hillbilly style. Some of the listeners clapped and stomped their feet along with him. The man let out a delighted whoop that made everyone cheer. Elvis grinned back at the man having fun.

In the middle row of seats Gladys and Vernon found some of their relatives. Gladys kissed everyone and the cousins said, "What'ya going to sing, Elvis?" Elvis blushed, but Mr. Cole patted him on the back.

On stage next, an old, wrinkled, stooped man started to sing in a squawking voice, his words unclear. "Boo!" someone shouted. "Drunk old coot." Abruptly the man stopped and left the platform. Elvis felt sorry for him.

Next came a girl in a pink dress who sang in a high voice while wringing her hands in front of her. She made Elvis tense.

"C'mon, you're next," said Mr. Cole, gently prodding him toward the platform. Elvis's stomach heaved. In a blur he made his way toward the front.

"Good luck," he heard his aunt say.

The announcer greeted him. "This little lad from East Tupelo doesn't have a guitar. Anyone want to accompany him?" No one responded. Elvis felt numb in his arms and legs. He stood in front of the microphone, which towered over him. The announcer strode out with a chair and made him stand on it. People snickered.

In a panic he recalled the day in school when he'd sung. He tried to picture Shep as he usually did, but it was hard. When his first words came, they sounded so loud in the microphone he nearly fell off the chair. But he braced himself and continued each sad verse, his voice small and plaintive in the big arena. Then he quickly climbed off the chair and ran back to the seats where his family were. Gladys hugged him. Vernon stood with his hands in his pockets, listening to the crowd's applause. Elvis was so glad it was over he didn't hear anything.

The contestants went on and on. Elvis relaxed and watched the others perform, amazed they could hide their fear. He daydreamed about the strutting palomino and glamorous woman, both of whom he wished he could watch forever. Nothing in his life was quite as wonderful.

Finally the announcer called time out to judge the contest. People stood up and stretched. Some went for coffee. Elvis shuffled his feet, making circles in the dirt.

"The winnah and first prize goes to Ring Childress from Mobile, Alabama." Applause followed the banjo player as he picked up his prize. "Second prize to the Green Sisters." The girls who had sung a duet hugged each other and ran up for their prize. "Third honor goes to the pupil from East Tupelo who broke our hearts with 'Old Shep' "

His family pushed him out in the aisle. Elvis felt mighty small as he walked up to the announcer who patted him on the head and gave him an envelope.

But he felt mighty big when he opened it and found five dollars and a free pass to all the rides at the Fair. "Wow, I'm rich!" he exclaimed, thinking of the ferris wheel, the dodgem cars, the roller coasters he could ride on now. For all this, performing surely had been worth it.

4: First Guitar

One day when Elvis was in school, he watched out the window as the sky grew browner and browner. Pretty soon the air became so thick he couldn't see the trees that lined the walk outside the window. "Sandstorm," said the teacher trying to be calm but still darting apprehensive looks toward the window.

What was happening? wondered Elvis.

After school Gladys waited for him as usual, only this time she looked harried and tense. "It looks bad, honey. I've closed up the house best I could. We're not going back there. We're goin' to Grandma Minnie's storm cellar. I bet she's down there already."

"Where's Daddy?" Elvis fell into step with her, as she hustled him toward the road.

"He's supposed to be building a barn. I went over to Aunt Pat's to telephone him but couldn't track him down. He'll probably hole out with the fellas at the cafe 'n' play cards and guzzle beer right through it all." There was a sharp edge in her voice. "But we're going to be safe."

First Guitar 23

Elvis grew afraid. Why did his daddy stay away? At least he could depend on his mother to know what to do. She stood by the road, eyeing the occasional cars as they emerged from the dust fog and waving her hand.

Finally a pickup truck stopped, "Where you headed?" asked the burly young red-headed driver. Gladys described Grandma Minnie's place. The guy said "okay" and Gladys pushed Elvis into the front seat between the two of them. The driver had huge muscular arms with a tattoo of a snake on the one closest to Elvis. Elvis shrank back into the seat, unsure whether this stranger would really take them to where they were going. At least his mother seemed sure.

She talked as they jostled along, enveloped by the dark sand drifting in the air. "Nineteen thirty-six — this whole area was nearly wiped out by a tornado. Remember? You're probably too young. Well, it feels the same now. The lull before the storm. God, I hope we don't have to live through that again. Everything was blown apart. Why, the roofs came right off the houses. No wonder the walls don't meet anymore."

"I gotta deliver this load to Memphis," their driver said. "I don't know if I'll make it." *Memphis.* That was the city where his daddy kept disappearing to, Elvis recalled. What was so great about it? Sometimes when his daddy talked about moving there to find a better job in a cotton plant, Elvis grew sad and angry because he didn't want to leave his friends and cousins in Tupelo. Sometimes he prayed that things would get better for his family so they wouldn't have to keep moving. He recognized the longing in his mother's face when she looked at magazines and stopped at pictures of living rooms with plush sofas and chairs and drapes, even though she'd say nothin' except, "Ain't that pretty now."

As they rode around Grandma Minnie's one-room shack to the back, they noted that the wind had increased. The tops of trees were swaying in the strong gusts. Elvis wanted to watch but his mother made him go down into the dark underground basement.

"Welcome to my parlor," said Minnie, who sat on a mat surrounded by candles, her thin legs stretched out in front of her. They sat down near her and leaned back against the wall. "I keep running upstairs to get something to do; otherwise I'd go crazy. Right now I'm sortin' leaves from the gum tree. Here, Elvis, I saved some sap for you."

Elvis put the soft ball into his mouth and chewed it like gum.

"Sorry, I don't have any Coke for you," she teased, reminding him of the day when he took a Coke from her porch without asking and his mother had spanked him and made him go back and apologize. He flushed.

Outside the wind rushed by. Something — probably a branch — clunked against the door. "Let me see what's happened," said Elvis.

"You stay right here, sweetie-pie. I got enough to worry about without you getting hit on the head by a flying saucer." Gladys laughed, Minnie too.

"Can I go get the radio then?"

"Well, okay," said Minnie. "Then we won't have to listen to the wind. But be careful now."

Elvis had to use all his might to push open the door. Outside he was amazed to see the wind bending the trees and bushes to the ground while the dust swirled. If only there was rain. He ran into the house and grabbed the radio from the table. Outside, as he fought to open the cellar door again, his hair and clothes were whipped around as though giant hands were trying to strip him.

He was relieved to return to the dark, cheery, cozy circle with his mother and grandmother. He turned the dial to a country music station, which came in surprisingly clear. The sound was twangy and lively. Elvis felt better right away.

The announcer reported severe storm warnings for the next four hours at least. Then came a sad ballad by Jimmie Rodgers that Elvis had heard before. He sang along softly with the singer. Grandma Minnie knitted. Gladys leaned her head back against the stone wall and closed her eyes. The songs filled Elvis's ears. He thought of others he'd learned, dimly aware of words coming back to him.

A blues program came on. There was a rough, rowdy song by Muddy Waters. Elvis could hardly understand the words, but the beat was strong and rhythmical. A haunting, crying song by B.B. King made Elvis's heart ache. Then an angry, screaming blues about the cruelty of life wrenched the boy. There was something about these songs that matched his deepest feelings of poverty, grief, and fear. These songs said what he thought but couldn't say. He sang with them because he loved their sound and wanted to make it part of him. In a storm they were the best comfort there was.

"Elvis?" his mother said dreamily.

"Yeah?"

"Remember that bicycle in the window you've wanted?"

"I sure do. Can we get it?"

"No, son, but there's a guitar in that window too. For thirteen dollars. How about that instead?" Her eyes begged him to accept.

"But, Mama, I want a bike so I can ride with my friends."

"I know, Elvis, but we can't afford it. We can't afford the guitar either, but I don't want you going around feeling bad."

Minnie said, "With a guitar you could play for yourself, like those other singers at the fair when you won the prize."

First Guitar 27

"Well, all right, but I'd sure like a bike."

"Someday maybe," murmured his mother.

Soon afterwards they heard no more whistling winds. Elvis slowly pushed open the door and saw the real world again. It was raining. The trees were still and, best of all, vividly clear.

True to her word, Gladys took Elvis to town and bought him the guitar. Elvis didn't know quite what to do with it, but his Uncles Johnny and Vester showed him how to play some chords. By himself on a hillside, he tried to pick out tunes he knew from church or the radio. He had fun fooling around with it, pretending he was like some of his favorite singing stars.

But then one Saturday his fears about leaving his friends and family in Tupelo came true. His daddy said they had to move, for they had no money to pay for their house. They were to pack up and leave for Memphis the next day.

5: Memphis

It was happening more and more often. Elvis closed his school locker with a bang, leaving all his books inside because he would need both hands free to fight. Chuck, the short guy with the broad chest and muscular arms developed from weight lifting, was waiting for him outside the door in the schoolyard. Last week it was a guy from the wrestling team, who had called him "Gorgeous George" because he didn't have a crew cut. Elvis had gotten his head punched around before he got away home.

This time Elvis knew he was being attacked for what happened last night at the movie theater where he worked as an usher. Sally had given him a couple of Mounds Bars as she did most other nights and the other usher, Chuck, snitched to the manager. Elvis was fired. Elvis was so mad he had flung his fist at Chuck's chest and swore at him. The manager broke up the fight, but Elvis knew from the moment he saw Chuck at school today that Chuck was going for him. He tucked himself in a corner and slipped out a back exit.

In Memphis, the Presley family had taken a

room in a boarding house. Three families shared the bathroom. In their room Elvis's mama cooked over a hotplate. There was no kitchen, only a table with chairs and a bed for each of them. The floor was stained linoleum. The plaster walls had holes. An electrical socket hung dangerously loose from the wall. His father had found odd jobs in a tool company and driving a truck. Gladys worked in a curtain factory and as a waitress. She was tired a lot, Elvis could tell, although she didn't complain. Elvis was scared for them.

Elvis remembered the first day he'd gone to Hume High School. He'd been amazed to find out there were twenty other high schools in the city. The brick building looked like a huge fortress. Windows were broken. Papers and cans were strewn on the bare ground where the grass had long ago been stamped out. His father had made him go in. On the way to the principal's office a bell rang and sixteen hundred kids suddenly jammed the halls, running, talking, pushing their way along. Elvis flattened himself against the wall of metal lockers. No one noticed him.

He had waited in front of the office to get put in an eighth grade class. The secretary seemed to forget he was there. In a flash he'd decided to leave and bolted through the front doors, running all the way home.

His mama was surprised when he came in. He explained what happened, and she said, "Well, honey, you got to go back. But let's leave it 'til tomorrow. I'll take a day off too and we'll get to know Memphis." They'd spent a wonderful day watching the steamboats and barges go up and down the Mississippi River. He was glad she wasn't mad.

The next day when he was finally placed in a class of thirty kids, he felt strange because he wasn't dressed the same as the others. The boys had on jeans and t-shirts. Elvis had worn black pants and a blue shirt his mother had gotten him at J.C. Penney's. He missed Tupelo badly. He decided that by being different he would in a way be loyal to Tupelo, his home. He was proud of his different ways and sometimes that caused trouble.

At home, when he was alone he had his guitar for company. He listened to the radio and learned to play his favorite songs. He admired the singers who could make him feel lonesome or happy, depending on the tune. There were plenty of famous singers and a lot of them came through Memphis or nearby Nashville.

After he lost his job as usher, his daddy got him another job after school from three in the afternoon until eleven-thirty in a metal factory. Elvis felt like a big man as he worked alongside the other men, even though he was much younger. The hours were long. He grew sleepy around ten, but he was glad to bring home the money to his parents. At least it helped a little.

His math teacher sent home a note saying he wasn't concentrating or doing his homework. So did his English teacher. Then a second warning came from the math teacher. Gladys said, "Elvis, you have to quit or you'll get sick. You could mow lawns instead." Shoot, he didn't care what he did, as long as he got the money to see a movie when he wanted.

Elvis thought school was a drag. The teachers spent most of their time trying to keep rowdy kids under control. Elvis wasn't much interested in any subject, except maybe shop where he learned about car engines and motorcycles. His mother had said he had to join the ROTC program so he could get a scholarship to college. He didn't care about more schooling, but he did like those uniforms. He had to watch it there too, because even when the boys went through their drills, all dressed alike, they razzed him about his hair and his being from a hick town.

He woke up dreading to go to school. It was not just the other kids that made him shy, but also the fear that when he came home, he'd find his mother and father gone, taken away because they were too poor. Even though his daddy found a steady job in a paint company, enabling the family to move to a Federally funded housing project, his parents talked about possibly being evicted. So although Elvis, for once, had his own room and an indoor bathroom just he and his parents shared, he had bad dreams about being helpless and alone.

Then one day he met Buzzie. There were many kids in the crowded housing project, some his own age. Buzzie lived in the same building as Elvis, and they started walking together to school. Nearby was a neighborhood of black people's shanties. Elvis and the boys from both places often met to play football. At last Elvis found some friends he liked.

6: Kickoff

Along with his friends Elvis tried out for the football team. The coach met with them and immediately put them through a difficult series of calisthenics and plays. He was a gruff man with a red face smooth as granite. Elvis, bending and running as hard as the other guys, said to him, "I may not be big and heavy but I am fast."

The coach eyed his lanky five-six frame. "Well, show up for daily practice and we'll see."

Elvis was elated when he was issued a uniform along with the regular team. His parents, though fearing he would get hurt, came to every game. Elvis sat the first few games on the bench and watched with total concentration the moves of his teammates. On the walls of his room he taped pictures of the great pro players.

Finally the coach put him in defense one quarter. Hume High was winning 21-6. He moved his hands quickly but was knocked down because of his lightness. Even though it jarred his insides, he liked playing and wanted to do more. He prayed he'd grow heavier.

One day during workout the coach said to

Elvis, "You cain't play ball with that hair in your eyes."

"I can see fine, sir. It doesn't bother me."

"Well, it bothers me. I don't like it. You either cut your hair or you don't play. Is that clear?"

Startled, Elvis put his hand to his slicked-back hair, which waved over his forehead but didn't even cover his ears. "But, sir, . . ."

"Look at the other boys here. Do they have hair as long as yours? No. Then why should you? You come back tomorrow with it cut if you want to play."

"Yes, sir." Elvis glumly left the field, ignoring the other boys who thought it was a big joke.

He walked toward Main Street where he was sure to find a barber. His feet dragged, his eyes studied the cracks in the sidewalk. He felt humiliated by the coach and grew angry. Why should the length of his hair matter in how he played football! The coach was threatening him just like the guys. Well, why didn't he just give in and get his hair cut? Then everything would be fine.

He stopped and stared in a windowpane of a shop. He took out his comb and smoothed his hair. He liked his hair. Yes, it was that part of him that was different. He'd look silly in a crew cut. "Shoot, man," Elvis mumbled, seeing a red-and-white barber's post up the street, "I don't want to go in there."

He turned around and headed home, shaking inside because he knew he risked giving up the one sport he loved. Maybe the coach would change his mind? He didn't sleep much that night.

The next day Elvis showed up for practice. "Get off the field," bellowed the coach, "until you get that hair cut."

For the rest of the season Elvis watched the team play from the sidelines.

He decided he would play it cool and be tough in his own way. He let his hair grow long enough to wave into a duck's tail in back. He got himself a yellow shirt, then a turquoise one and wore them unbuttoned at the chest. On Beale Street, where the jiviest black musicians bought their clothes, Elvis found a wild pair of pants with lightning streaks down the sides. He would have loved to buy a lot more.

He and Buzzie and some of the other guys went on dates together. Elvis used Vernon's old Plymouth. The boys liked to play the pinball machines whenever they had change. They especially liked to play at the concession stands in the amusement park.

One day when he and Buzzie were on dates with Sue and Martha, they were having Cokes and french fries at Oscar's. Elvis had the collar of his pink shirt turned up. He felt like a sharp dude in his shirt and black pants. He went over to the jukebox and put on Fats Domino singing "Blueberry Hill." As the familiar melody came on loud and clear, Elvis instinctively put his arms up as though he were strumming his guitar. Swaying with his body, he sang along with the throaty voice of Fats.

"Go man go," called out Buzzie. Elvis grinned at him but kept right on bopping and imitating the singer. Sue and Martha laughed. "He really can play the guitar," explained Buzzie to the girls. "I've seen him. Sometimes it gets so bad I can't shut him up."

Elvis sat down next to Sue and sipped his Coke. She said, "Why don't you bring your guitar to the school picnic next week?"

Elvis shook his head. "I cain't play, man. Hey, let's go somewhere and dance." He was sorry he had let himself go. He had only been fooling around.

At the end of his senior year, Miss Scrivener, his homeroom teacher, made an announcement: "This year I am the director of our variety show, which we put on every year to raise money for the Needy Student Fund. I need volunteers to sing, act, dance, recite a poem, anything. Now sign up. Don't be shy." She passed a piece of paper to Buzzie. Buzzie didn't sign it but handed it to Elvis. "Sign, man."

"Nah, the whole school will be there."

Red, another friend, overheard and said,

Kickoff 37

"Yeah, Elvis, sign up." He gave Elvis a friendly jab. Elvis thought how the fund had helped him out, so before he knew it, he signed his name. Afterward he was sorry, but Buzzie and Red held him to it.

On the night of the show Buzzie even loaned him a red shirt. Elvis was jittery. His parents, along with Memphis cityfolk, were in the audience. As he waited backstage in the auditorium Miss Scrivener darted around organizing the twenty kids who volunteered to perform. "There are so many of you," she was saying, "the one to get the most applause will be the only one to get an encore." The boys and girls milled around talking and joking; yet each of them was edgy, secretly hoping he or she would be the one to get the encore.

An hour passed as one act followed another. Elvis hid himself and his guitar near the folds of the curtain. For a while he amused himself by peering through a slit at the audience. He spotted the granite-faced coach and Chuck, the boy who had gotten him fired as an usher, and pretty Sue, and his folks, looking like they were having a good time. Boys on the football team who had jeered him were there. Elvis wondered how he could possibly dare to sing in front of them.

Not since that contest when he was nine years old had he sung in front of a crowd. He wanted to leave. His mouth was too dry. Suddenly Miss

Scrivener was there with her clipboard, "You're next, Elvis."

Elvis's knees were trembling as he stepped out into the light. He blinked fiercely. In a moment of panic through his head went all the country and western and blues he'd ever learned. He started off singing "I love you because you understand, dear/ ev'ry single thing I try to do." It was a love song that he sang softly and slowly, pausing just as the singer on the radio would.

Then it was time for the fast one — his favorite. But would anyone else like it? He smoothed back his hair, grinned shyly and threw himself into "Blue Suede Shoes." The audience clapped hard and long.

The applause rang in his ears. He thought of the times he had been mocked, how he had felt himself a stranger for so long, and now people were clapping. Excitedly he went off stage and burst out to Miss Scrivener, "They liked me! They really liked me!"

"You bet they did." She beamed.

When all the acts had been done, Miss Scrivener called to him and said, "It's you, Elvis. You get the encore." His heart seemed to leap in his mouth. What a great night it had been! He went out and sang "How Sweet Thy Spirit," an old spiritual he'd learned to love in Tupelo.

7: Present for Mama

Soon after Elvis graduated from Hume High School in 1953, his family was evicted from the housing project because they had not been able to keep up with paying the rent. Vernon and Gladys found a two-room apartment in a slum area. The familiar sickening sense of their poverty came over Elvis. He right away looked for work and found it on the assembly line at the Precision Tool Company. In the fall, Elvis found a better job driving a supply truck for electricians as they worked on the wiring of churches, schools, stores, and houses.

He walked to work, ignoring as much of the shabbiness around him as he could. Driving the truck was dull, but he realized he would have to work like his father at the odd jobs that came along and struggle just as hard to make enough money. The thought of at least fifty more years of low pay and long hours made him groan inwardly. Already he was tired and low-spirited when he came home at the end of the day, like his mama and daddy. He looked forward to evenings when he could ride around with his buddies or see Dixie Locke, a new girl friend who worked at the curtain store where he picked up his mother.

He still had his guitar and stacks of records he'd collected. Sometimes he joked around with his friends about being a singing star like Carl Perkins or Johnny Ray, but he knew it would never be possible for a poor boy like him. Still he often enjoyed daydreams and in his room hung pictures of his favorite singers. The memory of the variety show was still strong in him.

One day as Elvis was working with the electricians downtown, he saw a place called the Memphis Recording Service, where a sign invited you to make your own record — two songs for four dollars. Instantly he wanted to do it. Then he'd have a real record of himself that he could play along with his other favorites. He could hear what he really sounded like.

As soon as he scraped together the four dollars he hotfooted it down there. It was a Saturday morning. He carried his thirteen-dollar guitar with him. He walked into a small office, the walls crowded with posters of singers and the desk with papers. A woman sat at the desk talking on the telephone. Two men waited to talk to her.

Elvis' ears pricked up as he realized she was talking to a disc jockey. This was the closest he'd ever been to a real recording studio that made the records he heard on the radio. The two men who had been waiting told the woman they were looking for singing jobs. She told them there were none. They left dejectedly.

She turned to Elvis, who felt awkward with the big guitar in his lap. "What can I do for you?" she asked impatiently. The phone rang and she discussed the recording of a wedding. Afterwards she shook her head and said to Elvis, "You wouldn't believe how busy we are. I had it a lot easier when I was doing the program 'Miss Radio of Memphis.' Usually I'm not alone in the office. Sam is with me."

"I've heard that program a lot," Elvis answered, awed that he was talking to a real radio personality.

"Marion Keisker's my name. What's yours?" She stuck out her hand to shake his in a friendly way.

"Elvis Presley."

"What can I do for you, Elvis? Are you a singer?"

"Yes," he blurted, wishing he really was.

"What kind?"

"Oh, all kinds." He bluffed on the one chance in a million that she would be interested in him.

"Who do you sound like?" Her eyes were warm.

"I don't sound like nobody." He grinned in embarrassment, at a loss for what to say.

"Hillbilly?"

"Yeah, I sing hillbilly. I want to make a record."

"Everyone does. Well, the studio's being used right now but you can be next."

"Thanks a lot." It was difficult to wait. He jiggled the guitar on his knees. Finally four men in cowboy shirts and boots came out.

Marion said, "Okay, it's your turn now. They're through. Follow me."

She took him down a hall to a small room lined with spotted soundproof panels. A small window opened onto another room. The room was empty except for a stand-up microphone and a counter of taping equipment. "Now you sing here and I'll be in the other room cutting the record. I'll give you a hand signal through the window when to begin and when to do the other side."

"Okay." Elvis held his guitar in a ready position. The room was so quiet he heard himself breathing. No radio, no record, no other sounds were there to help him. He was afraid his voice would sound flat and mumbly. He'd planned exactly what he would sing, practiced the songs over and over again. Even so his adrenalin was racing as he stood poised to begin.

She signalled. He thumped the guitar hard, more to relax himself than anything. He launched into "My Happiness." Marion smiled at him when it was done and gave him a second cue. He threw his head back and plaintively sang the song about an unfaithful sweetheart. At the end he sighed and laughed, happy to have it done.

"I liked it. I think you've got something," Marion said, handing him the record.

"Thanks a lot." Elvis felt he floated out of there, his guitar under one arm and the amazing feel of his own record under the other. Marion's words stayed with him. Did she really mean it?

At home his mother was having a cup of tea when he came in. "Guess what?" He gave her shoulders a squeeze. "I have a present for you." He handed her the record.

"What's this, honey?"

"Here, let's put it on." He couldn't wait to hear it. The record turned and both held their breath in anticipation.

First came the guitar thumping. Elvis cringed. "Sounds like I'm beatin' on a bucket."

"Hush."

It was strange hearing himself. His voice was high but not as high as other hillbillies. Nor did he sound smooth as the pop stars he imitated. His voice seemed to screech and rattle along. Still it was a record of his voice. And there was his mama wiping away tears to "That's When Your Heartaches Begin."

He took his shoes off and put his feet up on

the table as they played it again and again. For a while, in their pleasure, both of them forgot their harsh life.

Some months later when he listened to the record with Dixie, he grew glum and sat with his arms across his chest, his mouth pouting.

Dixie said, "I wish I could have a disc. Why don't you make another one?"

Elvis' eyes lit up. "I will. I'm tired of this one. Good idea, hon." He gave her a kiss and then put on a stack of records for them to dance to.

Shortly before his nineteenth birthday in January, 1954, Elvis returned with four dollars to the Memphis Recording Service. This time, instead of Marion, a man with dark hair and bushy eyebrows greeted him. "I'm Sam Phillips, the owner. Can I help you?"

"Uh, I made a record a while ago and I want to cut another one."

"Sure thing." Sam led him to the studio.

Elvis sang a ballad called "Casual Love" and a country song, "I'll Never Stand In Your Way."

When he was done Sam said, "Give me your name and phone number." Elvis' heart flipped. He gave out Buzzie's number as his folks didn't have a phone. "You know," Sam recalled, "Marion told me about you. She taped your voice because she thought it was like the Inkspots. She said you were a white boy with black roots. She knows I think black folks sing the best rhythm and blues around, but they don't sell many records because the industry is controlled by prejudiced people."

Elvis listened as if his wildest hopes were about to become real. "Do you think I can be a singer?" he stammered.

"If anything comes up, I'll give you a call."

Elvis left, his imagination ablaze. Was there a chance he could get to sing somewhere? He knew Sam Phillips had turned him away just like the hundreds of other guys who had the same hope he did, but maybe he would call.

After a few weeks Elvis was sure he'd been forgotten. Still, he wanted to do something with his singing. One day he watched country and gospel singers record live music for a radio show run by disc jockey Bob Neal. One of the groups was the Blackwood Brothers Quartet. When Elvis heard they were looking for a replacement, he got up the nerve to ask if he could try out. It turned out they didn't want him for their group but they asked him to come to their all-night spiritual "sings," which they gave regularly in an auditorium.

Elvis wouldn't miss them. They reminded him of his singing in church in Tupelo, all that serenity and hellfire, joy and sin. He liked blending his voice with the others and learning new sounds. Occasionally he sang solos with the Blackwood Brothers harmonizing in the background. He would close his eyes, sway, and put all his feelings into the songs. He liked being appreciated, too, by others who had been singing longer than he had.

One Saturday Buzzie yelled from the door, "Elvis, telephone."

Elvis was eating a peanut butter and banana sandwich. He had on slacks but was shoeless and bare-chested. His hair was tousled. He'd just gotten up. "Who is it?" he asked, following Buzzie out the door.

"She said Mr. Phillips's office."

"Phillips!" Elvis ran past Buzzie to the phone. "Sorry to keep you waitin'," he panted into the receiver.

"Elvis, this is Marion. Sam has a song for you to try. Can you get down here right away?"

"Yes, ma'am!" Elvis hung up. "Whoopee! Hot dog!" he shouted at Buzzie, who looked somewhat shocked.

8: Gettin' It Together for Sun Records

Elvis ran back to his apartment only long enough to grab his shirt, comb, shoes, and guitar. He quickly hopped the streetcar that bore him to the Memphis Recording studios, also the home of Sun Records. He couldn't believe he had really been called!

Seeing his breathlessness, Marion quipped, "My, that *was* fast. How are you?"

"Fine. Mr. Phillips wants me?" He combed back his wild hair.

"It's a simple ballad with only one voice and guitar. Come on back." Marion stuck her head in an office and called Sam.

Sam handed Elvis some sheet music. "I can't read music," said Elvis, disappointed.

Sam, shaking his head said, "I should have known," and put on a tape of a song called "Without You." "Try it," said Sam.

Elvis tried to pull himself together. He hardly remembered the first word. He strummed, began the first line and faltered. Sam played the tape again while Elvis concentrated with all his might on the melody. The second time Elvis sang in a low baritone voice, crooning the words like Pat Boone, one of the popular singers at the time.

"Well, kid, that's not quite what I had in mind. Forget this one. Let's hear what *you* like to sing."

"I sure am sorry, sir." Elvis thought of the songs he knew best. They were imitations of popular hits and some gospel. Elvis sang them one after the other until two hours had passed and he was exhausted.

"You should try to be more natural. Feel free to be yourself. Let yourself go."

Elvis wasn't sure he understood what Sam Phillips meant, but he asked, "Do you think I would fit in a band?"

"There's a guy who plays guitar for me whenever I need a slot filled during a recording session. His name is Scotty Moore. He's got a hillbilly band called the Starlight Wranglers. I'll tell him about you."

"Gee, would you? Thanks." Elvis went home slowly, thinking that at least Sam Phillips hadn't told him to quit; still he was sorry he hadn't done better for his lucky break.

Several weeks went by, and Elvis was sure he had been forgotten again. To help himself forget his high hopes and routine work, he started dating a new young woman named Barbara Hearn. She was a good sympathizer. One night Elvis went to the movies with her. In the middle of the show he spotted Buzzie going down the aisle. "Buzzie," he whispered loudly.

"Hey man, I've been looking for you. Your mother sent me to tell you that Scotty Moore called."

Elvis ran out to call Scotty. Scotty's voice was friendly. "Come over to my house around two tomorrow." Elvis did not follow much of what happened in the rest of the movie.

He wore his favorite outfit to Scotty's — a white shirt, pink slacks, and white buck shoes. Scotty brought him into his living room and offered him a Coke. "My wife left the place to us," he said. Scotty was shorter and thinner than Elvis. He had light brown hair, blue eyes, and a wide smile. He seemed calmer than Elvis.

Scotty said, "Sam mentioned you the other day when I had lunch with him. How old are you and what do you do in your spare time?" They both laughed.

"I'm nineteen and I drive a truck. What about you?"

"I'm twenty-one and I work at a dry cleaner's. I guess you could say I'm crazy about music. At night my band plays in clubs around town."

"That's just what I want to do someday," Elvis said, wishing more than anything he could be in Scotty's shoes.

"Well, let's get started. I play acoustic guitar.

Tell me what you know and I'll try to follow."

Scotty stood holding his smaller guitar lightly. Elvis faced him with his guitar, playing chords as he sang music by hillbillies Eddy Arnold and Hank Snow, and black soul singer Billy Ekstine. Elvis was glad Scotty seemed happy doing the same songs.

While they were playing, another guy slipped in the door and listened. He was hefty, with curly dark hair. Scotty said, "Meet my neighbor Bill Black. He plays a mean bass fiddle." Elvis flashed him a smile that showed he was impressed to meet another musician.

Shortly after Bill left, Scotty laid his guitar down. "Well, that's all I have time for now. See you around."

Elvis wanted to ask him a bunch of questions but didn't dare. He mumbled goodbye and left, confused about whether Scotty really liked him or not.

A few days later Sam Phillips called. "Elvis," he said, "Scotty and Bill are willing to try an audition with you. Come on down and let's see what comes of it."

Elated and surprised that Scotty and Bill worked together, Elvis met them at the studio. They played. Sam said, "The fundamental thing for me is spirit and fervor. Try to develop more of a personal feel."

Scotty said, "Let's meet here every day after

work and see if we can't develop a style together."

"Okay by me," said Bill.

Elvis was willing to do anything, but he was nervous because he felt a lot hinged on his singing. He tried his best to imitate the popular style. Scotty gave him pointers.

After a week of practice Scotty asked Elvis to sing one night with his band at a local club. Elvis was thrilled. But still Sam didn't like their sound well enough to make a record. Sam played them tapes of other singers. "See," he would point out, "that's real. You can feel the hardship and loss there."

Another week of practice went by, then a month, then another month, and still Sam said, "Not yet."

One hot August night Bill said, "Maybe we are wasting our time."

Elvis felt his hopes sink. "Gee, not yet, fellas, we've been at it so long." He shot a worried look at Scotty.

"I've always felt we had something if only we could find it." He strummed lightly on the guitar. Elvis sang "I Love You Because." Bill plunked the strings of his bass. They all stopped abruptly, knowing the music sounded limp as a wet towel.

Elvis said, "Oh man, that has no juice in it. I feel like I'm fallin' asleep."

"Let's break for a Coke," suggested Scotty.

The three of them went outside in the night air. Having worked together for so long, there was no need to talk. Before them twinkled the blinking lights of cars and illuminated store windows. Horns honked. A couple walked by with their arms around each other. Overhead the moon loomed large, and millions of stars were very clear. Elvis felt lucky to be with Scotty and Bill, a real band, and waves of excitement went through him, despite their problems. Even the crickets were celebrating the summer night.

When he went back inside with the others, the night sounds and noises still throbbed within him, making his throat tingle. He felt rowdy. Recalling a song by Arthur Crudup, he grabbed his guitar and beat on it hard. Then he sang in a sarcastic tone: "Well, that's all right mama/ that's all right with you/ that's all right mama/ just anyway you do."

Bill quickly picked up the tempo on the bass and Scotty, looking curious, zipped along on his guitar. "Well, mama she done told me/ papa done told me too/ son, that gal you're foolin' with/ she ain't no good for you/that's all right mama...."

Suddenly Sam Phillips burst in the door. "What the devil are you doing?"

"Makin' a racket," said Bill, thumping madly away.

"Well, don't lose it," shouted Sam. "We'll record it."

Elvis looked stunned. As far as he knew, he wasn't even trying to sing, he was fooling around like he did when he was alone. That was the sound Sam had wanted all the time, and he had been so busy trying to copy others. He had always loved "That's All Right, Mama" because it was mean country blues and came from the gut.

The boys recorded the song. Sam said, "Now find another like it for the other side." It was about 3 A.M., so they broke up and went home so they could get up for work. Elvis was buoyant. They'd struck something new.

Night after night they practiced to find the groove again. Nothing worked. Finally Bill angrily thumped his bass and sang in a high falsetto voice an imitation of a hillbilly singing "Blue Moon of Kentucky." Scotty joined in with a twangy guitar, and then Elvis took over singing it a little faster, adding more bop to it.

"That's it!" exclaimed Scotty. "We've got it again. The secret is in the tempo."

They invited Sam to listen, and he immediately wanted to record it. He called in Marion. "Listen to the rhythm. It jelled."

"We're going to be run out of town for what we've done to these songs," mused Scotty.

Sam said, "I am offering you boys a contract."

Elvis felt his eyes brim with tears. Marion put her arm around him. He was going to have a real record. They celebrated with a cup of coffee.

Sam said, "I'm going to take this record over to Dewey Phillips, the disc jockey with the *Red Hot and Blue* program because he's the only white man brave enough to play black people's music. Maybe he'll take it on." Dewey Phillips agreed.

On the night that the record was to be played the first time, Elvis tuned in the radio for his parents and went to the movies. He was too afraid of their reaction to stay. They were sure to think he was too weird.

9: Starting Down the Road

Elvis was jerked out of his absorption in the movie by his mother who beckoned to him from the aisle. He jumped up. "Mom, what is it?"

"Elvis, you've got to come right away. Your song..."

Elvis felt like he did when he was a kid and about to get spanked. Was she mad? He followed her out of the theater.

Gladys explained breathlessly, "Dewey Phillips called. He wants you down at the radio station."

Elvis looked at her with disbelief. "What for?"

"I don't know, hon. He played the record and a little while later he played it again, saying that someone had called in and requested it. I would have done it myself if they didn't think I was showing favoritism." She smiled.

Elvis didn't know what to expect from Dewey Phillips as he entered the small radio shack. "Uh, hi," he said to the two men inside, one sipping coffee, the other with earphones on. "I'm Elvis Presley."

The one with earphones said, "Sit down. I want to interview you." Elvis's head rolled back in surprise. Phillips chuckled and added, "I've played your record seven times tonight already, and I have twenty more requests for it. I figured I'd better get you in here."

"I don't know nothin' about how to do it."

"Just don't say anything dirty." Phillips had him sit down in a chair near his control panel. "First, I need to know something about you."

Phillips asked him questions about his background and school, and as Elvis answered he grew more and more excited. People actually liked the record! And here he was being treated like a star. After a while Dewey Phillips said, "Well, thanks a lot, Elvis."

"I thought you were going to interview me?"

"I just did. The mike's been on the whole time." Elvis's face blanched. He had thought he was just introducing himself. He couldn't remember a thing he'd said.

A few days later Scotty called. "Sam says he's received 5,000 orders for the record."

"Holy mackerel!"

"That's the best I've done so far. The guys in my band are jealous. I think I am going to have to break with the Starlight Wranglers, so you, Bill, and I can work together." Elvis' spirits really soared. Everything was happening so wonderfully for him.

Sam Phillips told him that he'd gotten him a chance to sing one night at the Eagle's Nest, a ballroom where a band played. Elvis also sang with Scotty's Wranglers a few times. He sang popular love songs to mild applause. He was learning how to cope with the jitters in front of a crowd.

"That's All Right, Mama" became well known around Memphis but not much anywhere else. Sam Phillips said that the disc jockeys to whom he sent sample records just threw them in the wastebasket because the songs didn't fit into either the hillbilly or popular categories. Sam did get Elvis, Scotty, and Bill booked on the *Grand Ole Opry* and *Louisiana Hayride* Saturday night radio programs. Elvis and Scotty and Bill were excited because those programs were ones they always listened to.

Sam and Marion drove them to Nashville for the *Grand Ole Opry* show. Marion questioned Elvis about his hopes for the future, and he confessed that he hoped he could make more records someday and be famous.

The Grand Ole Opry was a large auditorium that packed in 3,500 people. Elvis, Scotty, and Bill couldn't get over that Hank Snow, one of the most popular country singers, would host the show and introduce them.

When it was their turn, they performed "That's All Right" and "Blue Moon of Kentucky." Afterwards the manager came up to Elvis and said, "I thought you were a hillbilly."

"I am — kind of."

"Don't sound like it to me. Don't waste my time coming around here again."

Tears filled Elvis's eyes as he turned away and walked aimlessly around. He eventually went to the car and just waited alone for the others to come. All the way home he didn't say much, so glum was he about the attack. He didn't know what style of singing would please everyone.

The format for the *Louisiana Hayride*, coming from Shreveport, was the same as the Opry. The boys would do the same two songs. Elvis was afraid of being criticized again, but he'd figured that he'd withstood plenty of attacks for his hair length in the past, so he should be able to take whatever else came his way. He was surprised though when a kid backstage approached him, fist clenched and threatening, "Just because you've got a record doesn't mean you're so great."

"Get lost, man," Elvis said as coolly as possible, although he was tense. The kid, seeing Scotty and Bill coming, turned away.

After Elvis, Scotty, and Bill performed, they were asked to come back every Saturday night for two years. "Wow!" said Elvis. "That's a whole lot better than we expected."

Scotty added, "The *Hayride* has a tour of

places in Arkansas, Louisiana, and Texas where we can be booked occasionally."

Barbara wasn't so keen on Elvis's being gone every Saturday night until he promised to take her along sometime. Every Saturday he and Bill piled their gear into Scotty's old Chevrolet and drove to Shreveport. They'd sleep in the car and eat in the cheapest places they could find. As they got to know more people, they received offers to perform in small spots.

Elvis was billed as the "Hillbilly Cat" or the "King of Western Bop." They agreed that Scotty would be their manager, since he was the most practical of the three, and that they would split what they earned — fifty percent for Elvis, twenty-five percent each for Scotty and Bill.

After some weeks of observing Elvis's travel, Gladys said to him, "Elvis, what about your plans for college? Aren't you getting sidetracked?"

"I'm gettin' to do what I always wanted to do. And it brings in a little extra money." He didn't say he was more ambitious than ever to be a singer.

She couldn't deny the extra money. She had been sick from overweight and strain, and Elvis's earnings had been needed even more.

Wherever Elvis was booked, he took a copy of their record to the local radio station and asked the disc jockeys to play it. He saw the way that they looked him up and down, judging his hair, the purple shirt, and white shoes. He tried to be pleasant, wanting to be friends with these guys in the music business. Sometimes they were interested in him, sometimes not.

One day before a show the three of them were having lunch. Elvis saw some cigars for sale and bought one. While he drank his vanilla shake, he puffed on the cigar. The heavy sweet-scented smoke filled his nostrils and pretty soon made him sick. Face sweating, he rushed to the bathroom, not quite making it on time, and getting vomit on his pink slacks. His only other pair of slacks were wrinkled at the knees from the hanger. He sang anyway, looking as much like a wreck as he felt.

Another time when Elvis, Scotty, and Bill were performing light, popular songs, they were booed off the stage. Driving away in the beat-up car, Elvis complained, "I sure hate to see people leave when I sing."

Bill said, "Well, they were expecting their bluegrass twangers."

"I think we need to do something different. We're doing the same old stuff like everyone else, and the thing is we're not like everyone else."

"Let's speed up the beat," said Elvis. "When we get real gone, then we're fine."

Their next chance came at Overton Park in

Starting Down the Road   61

Memphis, where an all-day country music show was being held. Elvis was feeling high because he knew the park well and their record had been popular with the cityfolk. Sam and Marion would be there, as well as his high school buddies and parents. The audience was packed and cheering, as one act after another took place.

Elvis prepared by dressing in a black sports coat with pink darts, black pants with pink pocket flaps and pink lightning bolts up the leg. His skin looked smooth and tanned. When it was his turn, he was ready and eager for the stage.

"Howdy," he said into the microphone and then introduced Scotty and Bill. They did their record tunes and then Elvis wailed with his eyes closed "I'll Never Let You Go, Little Darlin'." The audience became hushed. Then he signalled to Scotty and Bill to speed up their rhythm on the guitar and bass, and he let out a long "wel-l-l-l" and sang the song over from the beginning, shaking his hips and dropping his voice playfully. The audience erupted in screams and applause. At the end Elvis blushed and laughed, amazed that the people responded so much.

Sam had suggested that if they got an encore to do "Good Rocking Tonight," a very fast song. They threw themselves into it: "Well, I heard the news/ there's good rockin' tonight/ meet me in an hour behind the barn/ don't be afraid 'cause I'll do you no harm." Elvis noticed that as soon as he let his whole body go with the song, screams came from the crowd. He experimented a little to see what would happen. He threw one arm above his head and moved his knee in corkscrew fashion. "Well, we're going to rock, rock, rock/ aw come on and rock, rock, rock . . ."

In the final line — "we're going to rock our blues away" — he arched his pelvis and vibrated against the microphone, threw his head back and let out a high intense scream. Women jumped from their seats and shrieked louder than the music. Elvis was stunned at the commotion. The applause was far longer and more booming than any they had ever received.

In the wings Scotty and Bill were elated. Rock 'n' roll was obviously their thing. Sam came up and said, "There's your next record, fellas. And, great news, Bob Neal wants to meet with you about booking your shows. He arranges concerts through his radio station." Elvis knew him from the gospel music "sings" with the Blackwood Brothers.

Soon afterward, Bob wrote up a contract for his managing their performances and promotion. Gladys and Vernon had to sign for Elvis since he was legally underage. Bob cheerfully promised to get them a lot of action.

He did. It looked to Elvis that he could earn in

Starting Down the Road 63

one week as much as he did driving the truck for the company. Still, singing for a living was not reliable. He couldn't be sure of a job every week and then, if he did quit his job, he'd be out of money. His parents were very nervous about his thoughts of quitting. His friends saw his touring as more glamorous than it really was. He finally decided to take the risk and quit. He would now be a professional singer.

10: The Pivotal Point

Elvis kicked off the new year (1955) with the release of his second record, "Good Rocking Tonight," backed with "I Don't Care if the Sun Don't Shine." It became known in Memphis right away. Elvis was spotlighted in *Billboard Magazine* as someone who could appeal to country, rhythm and blues, and pop lovers. Bob Neal billed them as the "Blue Moon Boys" and made dates for them in school gyms and auditoriums in small southern towns. One such town was Stamford, Texas, population 4,000, mostly rural.

While Scotty drove their second-hand white Cadillac there, Elvis tried to sleep but couldn't. He thought about Barbara, how he wanted to marry her so he wouldn't lose her, but his mother had said he was too busy to make a girl happy. Suddenly, as a joke and to ease the tensions of the drive he threw his shoe out the window and made them all stop and go look for it. "Aw, come on," sighed Scotty who was used to Elvis's fooling around, "not again."

Finally around the middle of the afternoon

Elvis, whose turn it was to drive, entered Stamford and rode slowly around the center square of town, checking it out. Elvis hung his arm out the window, smiling laconically at anyone who caught his eye. Like many of the towns they went to, there was only one restaurant and one movie house. Bill said, "Guess we won't starve here but I don't see where we're going to put up for the night."

"Go out further," Scotty said. "Maybe there's a motel."

Elvis said, "Maybe they'll run us out of town after tonight. Don't look like anyone's under a hundred here."

"Don't worry," Bill said, "the teenagers will find you. They may live spread out on these ranches but news travels fast. The disc jockeys know how to reach 'em and sell tickets."

They found a motel on the outskirts of town and then walked to the Superdog, where they ate chicken-fried steak and french fries.

Back at the motel Elvis laid out the white pants and shirt and shoes he planned to wear later. He put his guitar over his shoulder and strummed a few chords, shaking his shoulders and legs loosely. Scotty and Bill went right on unpacking their gear. Elvis set the guitar down and flopped back on the bed. His feet jiggled. He laid his arms at his sides but it was not long before he raised them, snapping his fingers, nodding his head to some rhythm inside of him. He said in exasperation, "Man, how long do we have to wait?"

Scotty smiled, accustomed to his restlessness. "Another hour and then we can go over there and set up."

Bill turned on the television. News came on. He changed the channel to a western movie. They watched that until Elvis sat up and threw a pillow at Bill. Bill threw one back and then Elvis pounded Scotty, who grabbed a pillow, and pretty soon all three were pummelling each other and laughing. Then, facing each other on the floor, they grew as quiet as they had been noisy.

Elvis picked up his guitar again, twiddled the strings, and sang softly: "I've been travelin' over mountains/ even through the valleys too/ baby, running all the way/ tryin' to get to you." He stopped strumming. "Boy, I hope I remember the words."

"They'll come back to you," Bill said, nervous himself.

Scotty went out to get some Cokes.

They proceeded to get dressed. Bill and Scotty put on their black cowboy shirts and pants with white leather belts and ties. They wore cowboy boots. Elvis, dressed all in white, seemed to shine like a star already. Freshly shaved, he combed his brown hair back at the sides, but a lock on top kept falling out of place onto his forehead. He looked in the mirror and gave himself a sidelong smile. He admired the dazzling white clothes. They made him look like he always wanted to. In them, he didn't feel quite as nervous.

Bill drove them to the high school auditorium. The lights were on in front but no cars were in the parking lot. Scotty went in the front door and came back a few minutes later with an old janitor who helped them carry their equipment backstage. Elvis said, "Coming tonight, Pop?"

The old man chuckled. "You hillbillies?"

"Not exactly. I'm a rockabilly," Elvis cracked. "Hey, bring your family. Be my guest."

"Thanks a lot," the man said, turning on the lights.

Scotty dragged the sound boxes for his steel guitar on stage, while Bill set up his stool and huge bass fiddle. The janitor turned on the microphone, which Elvis tested with popping sounds. He sang a few lines of a song to the empty row of seats. Without any people his voice sounded flat and dull, he thought.

Two men came into the auditorium. "The principal and Tom, the DJ," said Bill. "I'll check with them." When he came back, he said, "They've only sold about twenty-five tickets. Jees, doesn't anyone know when good music comes to these parts!"

Scotty said, "They'll sell more at the door before we start. You'll see."

He was right. From behind the closed curtain on stage they could hear people coming in and, peeping through the curtain folds, they saw about fifty people who had paid fifty cents to at-

Singing with Scotty Moore on guitar, D. J. Fontana on drums, Bill Black on bass

tend. There were grownups and many teenaged girls in blouses and full skirts with petticoats underneath. Some kids told about hearing Elvis in his last show in Abilene. "You've never seen anything like him," someone said. "He's a real live wire."

When the curtains on stage parted, the curious audience saw Bill plucking the strings of his bass and acting as if he was going to ride it like a bucking bronco. Scotty grinned at his clowning. They played duo for a while and then Scotty announced, "Here is Elvis Presley — the Bopping Hillbilly, the Memphis Flash!" They played a fast crashing piece to usher Elvis on stage. Their plan was to start off with a bang.

Twenty-year-old, lithe, handsome Elvis came on and stood before the people. He gave them a casual, sensual smile. Despite his nervousness he looked loose and at ease. He braced his legs and burst into "Long tall Sally." "Gonna tell Aunt Mary about Uncle John./ He claims he has the misery/ But he's out havin' fun./ Oh, Baby-yes, Baby Whoo-oo Baby./ Havin' me some fun tonight." His shoes beat the rhythm. He clapped his guitar and waved his arm at the end of a chord, as if the song dangled alive at his fingertips. The audience was so stunned they almost forgot to clap. Elvis wanted them to have fun.

Then he sang "I Don't Care If the Sun Don't Shine," which went slightly slower but still rollicked along. This time the audience clapped right away. The smiles on people's faces made Elvis relax more. The audience responded appreciatively. He laughed, his mouth curling to the side, and kids laughed with him. He joked about the microphone, the way he could make it flop around, like a wet noodle.

When he sang sweet sad "Old Shep," caressing the words, a hush came over everyone. He sang rowdy "Lawdy Miss Clawdy" hard, letting his body quiver with the music. Sweat gathered on his head and neck. He pursed his lips sexily. The music seemed to set his body free. He was happy because he could feel that he'd gotten the crowd moving and feeling good too. He wanted to give them all he had.

The applause was so fervent at the end he sang three extra songs. The curtain was closed.

"That was great," Bill said. "They were really warmed up."

"We've hit our stride," Scotty mused.

Suddenly a crowd of girls swarmed around Elvis backstage, clamoring for his autograph on scraps of paper. At first he felt funny about signing, but he liked their eagerness. He always wrote "Yours, Elvis" and talked to them. They reminded him of his high school friends. One girl asked him to stay forever. "At least come to our romp-stomp dance hall."

"I cain't, honey, I got to move on." He put his arm around her.

Another asked, "When are you coming back?" Then another, "What's your address?"

Elvis did his best to answer questions, while Scotty and Bill dismantled the sound equipment and cleared the stage. They were beginning to get used to Elvis's wild effect, especially on females.

The janitor began turning off the lights, forcing everyone to leave. "He's the cutest thing I've ever seen," a girl groaned as she left. "He's disgusting. Probably a dope fiend," her boyfriend replied. "This has been the most exciting night of my life!" exclaimed another. "I've just got to see him again, no matter what my parents say!"

And so it went. As Elvis and Scotty and Bill blazed their trail across the South, they attracted more and more attention. Newspaper and magazine stories appeared. Kids requested their radio stations to play Elvis's records. Occasionally a successful manager of other singers, named Colonel Tom Parker, helped Bob Neal book shows for the threesome. They made a third record to take around with them: "Milkcow Blues Boogie" backed with "You're a Heartbreaker."

One morning after a performance in Wichita Falls, Texas, Elvis, Scotty, and Bill were having breakfast in a coffee shop when three girls came over to their table. Elvis looked at them curiously. Each one had made herself up prettily and seemed too breathless to speak. Elvis smiled sidelong and said, "Sit down." The girls' eyes were fixed on him, and he felt himself turn red but discovered he liked attention just the same.

"Elvis," the girl in pink shorts said, "we heard you sing last night. This was our second time. We want to start a fan club for you."

"A fan club — for me?" Elvis exchanged glances with Scotty and Bill.

"Yeah," said the one in jeans. "We got these cards printed up." In front of him she put a stack of one hundred small cards that said 'This is to certify that _____ is a member in good standing of the Elvis Presley Fan Club.' "We want you to sign them to make it official."

"Sure thing." Elvis reached over, took a pen from the one with long black hair, and started signing. "Are you all from around here? What made you think of this idea?" Scotty and Bill watched and sipped their coffee.

"Because we adore the way you sing. You make us feel so good. We have all your records. We talked to the DJ at our station."

Elvis chuckled and the girls giggled.

"We want to send our members a picture of you."

"I'll mail you some", said Elvis. "Write down where I should send them."

"That would be great!" The one in pink rather

shakily wrote out an address and handed it to him. "Thank you." She looked on the verge of tears.

Elvis said, "I like it here, but now we have to head back to Shreveport for the *Hayride*."

"Oh, we listen every week — when we can get good reception."

"We done burned out two cars already goin' back and forth." When Scotty and Bill paid the bill, the girls rose to go. Elvis stood and put his arm around them. "Thanks for doin' all that you do. I really appreciate it."

"Oh well, we really love you, Elvis," the girl with long hair said.

"Bye." Elvis waved to them but before he turned away he saw the one in jeans grab the toast left on his plate and the napkin. Now ain't that somethin', he thought.

When he got back to Memphis, he went to a photography studio to have pictures made to be sent to not only the girls in Wichita Falls, but to many other fan clubs that were starting up.

Elvis decided to celebrate by buying a pink Cadillac.

11: Elvis Is Pressed — at Sun Records and Elsewhere

Elvis met with Scotty and Bill and Sam Phillips at Sun Records for their fourth recording session. He was nervous because he had no idea of anything new to sing. "Well," said Sam, "what songs do you plan to do?"

Bill shrugged. "We talked it over but Elvis couldn't decide."

"How about a spiritual?" Elvis joked, although he really wanted to record a gospel song. He began to sing "Swing Low, Sweet Chariot."

"Sounds like a funeral," said Sam. "I can't believe you guys aren't prepared. No one walks in here and records without being fully rehearsed."

Scotty picked at his guitar. "We've been doing some new songs on the road that are going over big."

"Well, let's hear them."

Elvis, Scotty, and Bill went through three songs. Sam observed, "You don't seem to have much zip today. What's the matter?"

Publicity photo for fan clubs

"Aw gee," Bill griped, "Bob Neal wants us to go on salary and give Elvis a bigger cut. It kinda took the wind out of our sails."

Sam nodded. "I've heard this before when my other singers have become stars." He put his arms around Scotty's and Bill's shoulders. "You guys would be crazy to break up just when things are starting to pick up for you." Elvis was leaning against a table and feeling bad. He hated this fight with his pals, but he knew he was the one for whom the crowd hollered and started fan clubs. He'd agreed with Bob.

Scotty said, "It's just hard to get used to. I have a family to support on what I make."

Billy added gloomily, "And Colonel Parker's been telling Bob and us we'll never get anywhere sticking with you here at Sun Records."

Elvis threw Sam a pained glance. Sam was his hero. Elvis was totally grateful to Sam for giving him a chance and recording "That's All Right." He didn't think he could ever leave Sam, but it was true he'd listened with interest to what Parker said about getting big.

Sam paced as he answered. "That figures. Parker said that about Eddy Arnold too. The fact is I find and build up guys like you and he likes to take them away. You guys would be nowhere without me. Now you're famous all over the South."

"Bob wants us to fly up to New York City to

Elvis Is Pressed 77

try out for Arthur Godfrey's Talent Scout television show," Scotty said.

"Go ahead. Try your luck up North. New York is full of guys who are hard to please. You'll find out."

"Let's get to work," Elvis pleaded. "All I really want to do is sing. I thank the Lord that we were brought together." He picked up his guitar. "Come on fellas, let's warm up with our strongest numbers."

They did "Long Tall Sally" and "Blue Suede Shoes." Elvis, panting afterwards, felt much better.

Sam said, "You can't record those. They're on the jukebox by other people. Too bad you don't write your own songs."

"I can only listen and do what I like," said Elvis.

"I can play you some demonstration tapes of songs that have come in. I have a lot of blues you'll like." While Scotty, Bill, and Elvis listened, Sam went out for sandwiches and Cokes to get ready for what he knew promised to be a long evening ahead.

Elvis concentrated hard on what he heard. He replayed portions and tried to capture the words and sounds. Often he garbled the words and made up sounds instead. Then he'd laugh, enjoying the things he could do with his voice. He was a sucker for rock n' roll blues. Scotty and Bill had a hard time following him.

When Sam returned, they were working on one called "You're Right, I'm Left, She's Gone." Sam said, "Hey, that sounds great! You guys are so much better than you used to be. Stronger. More sure of yourselves.

Considerably heartened, they continued polishing the tricky tempo of the fast-paced blues song. When Elvis thought it sounded right, he said "Okay, let's record it." It was about 9 P.M.

They took a break, but Elvis couldn't relax. He listened to more tapes, strumming along on his guitar, searching for those songs that appealed to him. In the beginning he had depended on Sam or Scotty to suggest what to sing. Now he had a strong feeling for what sounded right. He knew if he liked the song he had a better chance for making it come alive. Often he needed to close his eyes to get that feeling. The song had to take him over. In a way, he felt that singing was a way of reaching God. So when he practiced, he tried to get in touch with the spirit of the song. He couldn't explain it, but he knew Scotty and Bill knew what he was doing and respected it.

He found a song he thought was funny. It went: "You may go to college/ you may go to school/ you may drive a new Cadillac/ but don't you be nobody's fool . . ." He changed the words "new Cadillac" to "pink Cadillac." He still loved his pink Cadillac, but it had caught fire on the road while he was driving to a show. He had had just enough time to get his clothes and guitar out before the thing burned out. Now he had an order in for a pink one with a black top, which he promised to take much better care of. He adored Cadillacs. They made him feel like the big singing stars he'd seen around Memphis. As soon as someone became famous, he bought a Cadillac. It was the sign of success.

The group tried out some other songs. Sam looked tired, but Scotty and Bill kept plugging along. Elvis perspired. His hair dropped in his face. He sat on a stool, thrumming his guitar, rocking his head, and hunching his shoulders to the beat. A guitar string snapped and popped up like a strand of spaghetti.

Elvis changed it and started up again. "There's no one screamin'," he joked. "I can't tell if I'm any good or not." Bill laughed.

Scotty said, "Let's go back to 'Baby, Let's Play House'."

During the instrumental part Elvis closed his eyes. He felt at last warmed up for the song. "Well, you may go to college," he began. Then his voice dipped into a stream of "well, dee-dee-dee-dee, dee-dee-dee-dee/ Come back, baby/ I want to play house with you." They went through it again and this time he improvised on the word "baby," repeating it in a low sexy voice. At the end he laughed. His fooling with it had put some jive into it. "Let's do it that way," he said.

Scotty and Bill agreed. Sam said, "Well, you guys are probably the first in history to walk into a recording session unprepared but you certainly do have fun."

It was about 2 A.M. when they finished. Scotty left to go home. Bill went to get something to eat. Elvis was so keyed up that he knew he'd never fall asleep. He decided to go looking for some friends. He'd love to have a ride on a motorcycle and go zooming around town.

The next week Elvis, Scotty, and Bill joined the Hank Snow Jamboree tour for three weeks. They were included with a big list of singers and played at coliseums where the crowds were bigger than they were used to. Colonel Parker helped Bob Neal arrange this for them. After that they went to New York City to try out for the Talent Scout show. Elvis was dazed by his first airplane ride and visit to busy, crowded New York City. He was rejected by the show.

They came back for another tour with big names in Florida, arranged by Colonel Parker. Sometimes they took along with them a new drummer they'd befriended at the *Hayride*—a man named D. J. Fontana, who made Elvis's music backup even stronger. People said Elvis stole the show; and because no one wanted to follow his act, he was put on last. The "Baby,

Let's Play House" record was the first one to get listed on a national sales chart of country music. Bob Neal wrote a story about him and put his picture with Scotty and Bill's in the *Hillbilly and Country Hit Parade Magazine.*

Elvis grew shaky sometimes when he thought about his good luck. Sam had them back for another recording session. After another long night "Mystery Train" and "I Forgot to Remember to Forget" were made.

One night after a show, Elvis finished as usual by signing autographs and talking with a few girls who got in the dressing room by claiming to be in his fan club. He walked out to the parking lot with his gear to meet Scotty and Bill. A guy from another car hollered and waved, "Hey Elvis, come here." Elvis thought someone wanted an autograph and went over. As he bent down to the window, the guy hauled back his fist and slammed Elvis in the face. He drove off, burning rubber behind him.

Elvis's nose felt battered. His eyes hurt. He reeled for a few minutes before he realized what had happened. Then he was angry. That creep is going to get it. He found Scotty and Bill and told them what happened. "I've got to find him and pay him back. Come on!"

Elvis drove around town for hours but couldn't find the car. Finally he decided to give up. He determined he'd better take lessons from his friend Red West, a boxer, on defending himself against jealous guys.

Shortly after that, at another show, Elvis was mobbed before he got off the stage. Hordes of girls stormed the aisles and leaped on stage before he finished his bow. Elvis was so surprised he froze. "Elvis!" they screamed. "Don't go. We love you!" A tall girl grabbed him around the neck. It hurt and he struggled loose. Another clutched him, refusing to let go of his shirt as he pulled away. The buttons were torn off. He got scared then. He was going to be crushed if he didn't get away. The crowd was too big and too close. Someone was untying his shoelaces. As he fought with his arms to get through the pressing bodies, he felt himself topple over, his shoes taken off. The din around him was scary. His skin was scratched. He felt like he was being gobbled up alive. He covered his head with his hands.

Just then Scotty and Bill broke through with two guards, who pulled everyone off. Elvis scrambled up in the remains of his clothes and limped away. Helping him, Scotty said, "We've got to get out of here fast."

When they reached the car, Elvis laid his head back on the seat. Bill said, "Boy, this is really bad. You could be messed up good. We'd better get police protection from now on."

After Elvis told his parents what happened,

Gladys begged, "Oh Elvis, take a rest. You need it. Colonel Parker came by for a visit and he said his family has a farm for you to stay at. I think he's right. You're going to burn yourself out."

"Oh, Mama," Elvis laughed, tickled by her and the incident, "the last thing I want is a rest."

12: Big Business

After one big weekend Elvis had slept until after noon and now, relaxed, he was waxing his own sweet Cadillac. He'd made the black top shine so he could see his reflection in it. The pink body was light and creamy as a strawberry milk shake. The chrome gleamed. Inside were soft plush seats. The car had class. Sometimes he dreamed of getting a purple or yellow car to go with other of his clothes too, but he was very satisfied with this sleek handsome pink and black baby.

Colonel Parker was coming over to talk to him and his parents. He was nervous about that. He would have liked to call Barbara and talk to her about everything, but he couldn't anymore. They'd broken up because he was away every weekend and he guessed she had other boyfriends now. His going on the road had changed a lot of things. He was twenty pounds heavier, largely from eating hamburgers, french fries, and ice cream milk shakes most of the time. He couldn't sleep for more than short periods at night. He'd wake up worrying about songs, performances, and people.

"Pretty nice, eh boy?" a voice broke into his reverie. It was Tom Parker, wearing a Stetson hat and smoking a cigar.

"Howdy," said Elvis, his stomach muscles at once tingling with tension. He couldn't get used to someone as important as Parker taking an interest in him.

"I'm getting ready to set up camp in New York City and invite the boys from RCA over for a chat." He patted the Cadillac.

"Well, come on inside. My dad just got home from work." Elvis's brain whirled. He knew that RCA was the biggest recording company in the country and that Parker wanted to have him work with RCA rather than Sun. All his fears about leaving Sam were stirred up.

Vernon and Gladys shook hands with Parker and gave him some iced tea and their best chair. Gladys sat down stiffly and fanned herself with a magazine. Even in her sundress she was perspiring. She'd grown very heavy and her eyes had a sunken, tired look. Her feet were swollen too. "Whoo-ee," she said, "it's too hot even for fish on a day like this."

Vernon said, "I'd like to be fishing now." He sat with his arms folded on the corner of a table. He chewed gum, a little unsure how to treat the businessman Parker.

"Me too," said Parker. "Let's go together sometime. Now I want to talk over something important." While he explained why he wanted Elvis to join RCA, Elvis leaned against the wall, hair over one eye, thinking about how much he had worshipped Sam Phillips ever since the day he'd met him. He also felt no confidence in his ability to move up to the bigger company.

Colonel Tom Parker had a reputation for being a great show business hustler. His uncle owned a pony circus and from his boyhood Tom Parker learned how to make up carnival acts. Sometimes he sold hot dogs. The buns were a foot long but there was no more than a little piece of wiener sticking out at each end. Another time he stood a whole herd of cows at the exit flap of the circus tent, so that when the people left, they could choose between walking through fresh manure or paying Parker a quarter for a pony ride out. Parker had learned to be clever about making money because the carnival life was poor. He got his clothes from trash cans. As he got older, he expanded into promoting country singers instead of circus acts.

Stories about him were told constantly. Supposedly he'd scheduled singers in two different towns on the same night. As soon as the singers finished at one place they'd rush over to another place to do another show. That way Parker made twice the money each night. One night when a singer was too sick to perform, Parker substituted "Dancing Chickens." He hid a hotplate under the straw of a chicken cage. Then he plugged it in. The chickens leapt up and down to keep from burning themselves while musicians played "Turkey in the Straw."

But Parker was known as a pioneer in country music. Before him only radio stations arranged shows for singers. He ignored them and got organizations like feed companies to pay the costs for a show. Now he was saying, "I've gotten contracts for others at RCA. Your boy, Elvis, in my opinion is ready for national fame. He's been a local success. Now it is time to move on. Why, I even suspect that in the not too distant future we could get a movie deal for him."

Elvis's heart flipped. the movies were more than he'd imagined. He was already overwhelmed by the audience reaction he was getting wherever he went now in the South. The last two records were really selling well. He had gotten more than he'd ever desired, but still he was tempted to think that he could be liked by even bigger audiences in the rest of the nation. "But," Elvis said pouting, "I'm recording with Sun. I have a contract with Sam."

"He'll sell it," said Parker. "If I can get RCA to pay enough, he'll be glad to."

Vernon said, "If it means more money, Elvis, I think you should do it. God knows we could use it." Elvis considered how much he'd like to buy a house for him and his parents.

Parker said, "I want to be your manager, boy. Put yourself in my hands and we'll go far. You're the hottest thing that's come down my pike, and I keep a sharp eye out."

Gladys said, "Colonel Parker understands how we feel, honey. He's one of our kind. He knows you've been overworked. He says you would do less shows for more money with him managin'."

Parker said, "Yeah, for instance I'd cut the *Hayride* so you were free on Saturday nights."

To Elvis everything was moving too fast. In less than a year he had five records when before he used to think he'd never get to make one. He had real fans who clapped and cheered for him. He loved singing. It was more like playing or having fun than working. Still, being more famous and receiving top billing in a show were things he hankered for.

Parker pulled out his wallet and handed Vernon two hundred dollar bills. "Take it. Have a vacation. A token of things to come." Vernon turned red from surprise, but he took the money. Parker turned to Elvis and said, "I know what you're thinking, but you have to look out for yourself too. Sam Phillips has a good studio here in Memphis, but it isn't large enough to distribute your records nationally. Unless you break away, you will never be more than a regional country singer."

Elvis mused, "But will the big city slickers like me?" He already knew he'd decided to take the risk and find out.

Parker drew up an agreement, empowering him to act for Elvis, which Elvis and his parents signed. When it was done, Elvis was afraid things would be different with Scotty and Bill. He dreaded facing Bob Neal and Sam.

When Parker came back from New York, he told Elvis RCA was willing to pay Sam Phillips the fantastic sum of $35,000 for the rights to Elvis's singing and $5,000 to Elvis himself as a bonus.

Elvis was amazed at the money and even more at Parker's ability to get it. He told Bob Neal, who cheerfully agreed to Parker's taking over for him. "I always knew it would happen sooner or later," he said. He told Scotty and Bill. They felt like he did, enthusiastic but regretful toward Sam. Elvis told Sam. Sam said he'd think it over. Marion was upset.

Seeing Elvis stew, Vernon said to him, "Sun Records has gotten a lot from you. They owe you something too."

"Knock it off," Elvis retorted. "Sam and Marion are my friends. They had faith in me."

In time Sam called and said, "I don't want to sell your contract, but I've been thinking how hard it is for me to record you — those long sessions, all that wasted tape — while you work out your style. And it's true I can't handle a huge volume in orders. I think you've outgrown me. I'm accepting RCA's offer. Good luck."

"Thanks a lot, Sam. I'll always be grateful."

"Sure thing, Elvis. See you around."

On January 5th, 1956, shortly before his twenty-first birthday, Elvis was to cut his first record for RCA. He drove to their nearest studio in Nashville with Scotty, Bill, and D.J., the drummer. He had no idea what to sing, as usual, even though he didn't expect RCA to tolerate the cutting up the way Sam did at Sun. On an impulse he'd asked the Jordonnaires to come. They were four men who sang spirituals on the *Grand Ole Opry*. Elvis knew they could improvise the way he liked.

The studio was located in a former church, which made every sound seem like it came from an underground cave. Colonel Parker and other RCA executives were there. Elvis, wearing a proper suit but no tie, shook hands with everyone. Steve Sholes, an RCA man, said, "We brought a piano player and another guitarist. If you want more backup, we can arrange it."

Elvis was impressed that they were trying to please him. He said, "Well, first we got to get to know each other." He was nervous about doing well in front of these businessmen. The atmosphere in the Sun studio had been more personal and casual.

The band, the largest he'd ever had, went through some songs with him. Elvis felt his body and voice tighten with the officials watching him. He knew he'd never get anywhere if he let himself get this bothered. He had to stay loose, keep it fun, in order to sing right at all. He began working on "I Want You, I Need You, I Love You," then "I Was the One." The first was a lively love song; the second a desperate lament. In both the Jordonnaire's hummed and "ooohhhed" and "aaahhhed" softly to round out his words. The guitars came on strong. Bill's bass was less audible than when they'd played before.

In "Heartbreak Hotel" a jivey piano sound was added and the Jordonnaires removed. Elvis sang with all the loneliness he felt about losing Barbara: " ... so if your baby leaves you/ and you've gotta tell the tale/ just take a walk down Lonely Street/ to Heartbreak Hotel/ where you'll be so lonely/ so lonely you could die."

"Whew," said an RCA official. "That'll have them wringing their handkerchiefs."

Another asked him, "Do you protect your voice in any way? I'm serious. Get some advice from a doctor. With all that singing you do, you've got to keep it lubricated to keep from straining it."

When Elvis heard the songs played back, he thought they were the best he'd done so far. His voice had more range, more fluidity, more rhythm. It was becoming more pop and blues than country. He said to the Jordonnaires, "If any of these songs go big, I want you to record with me all the time."

"Sure thing," came the doubtful answer.

Colonel Parker, Steve Sholes, and the other men wanted to go to a restaurant. They asked Elvis to join them.

"No sir, I can't sit down right now." He was raring to go have fun and was relieved that Colonel Parker could take over business for him. Elvis found Scotty and Bill. "Come on, let's drive around Nashville."

They found an amusement park where there were ball-tossing games, rifle-shooting, pinball machines, and pool. For a couple of hours they played games. Elvis won three stuffed animals throwing a ball at wooden bottles, and then the concession owner wouldn't let him play again.

"Let's go to a movie," Elvis urged. They were in a strange city with a strange recording studio and it just seemed right to try to recapture their old familiar closeness and fun.

13: Television

Elvis was spending more time living out of a suitcase than at home. Even though he enjoyed seeing new places and people, especially the pretty young women, he still called home every night to tell his parents about what was going on. He also started bringing along some of his Memphis friends, like Sonny West, who thought his life on the road was pretty special. That way Elvis kept familiar faces around him and also got relief from some of the driving and other odd chores.

One day in a meeting, Colonel Parker told Elvis that he'd arranged for Elvis to appear on television six different Saturday nights for $1,250 apiece. "If we're successful on TV, we might have a chance to get to Hollywood," Parker said.

On January 28, 1956, Elvis and the boys flew to New York City. Parker met them at their hotel, and they all went to the television studio for the Dorsey Brothers Show. Elvis bit his fingernails. Parker said, "On TV people can see and hear you. On radio they just hear you. You, Elvis, they need to see!" Elvis agreed, though nervously.

He and Scotty and Bill were first taken to the makeup room, where their faces were coated with a tan cream. Tommy and Jimmy Dorsey sat down to explain the way their half-hour talent show worked. They told Elvis he would have no time to warm up with Scotty and Bill because the show was starting in ten minutes.

He had to step immediately out onto a floodlit stage. In the audience were very few people. To relax, Elvis tried to imagine more viewers sitting in their homes watching their sets. As he sang his two songs his eyes searched the TV camera as if for some response, which was impossible to get. It was hard to put much feeling into the songs.

Soon after it was over he, Scotty, Bill, and D.J. flew to their next concert date.

The next time Elvis appeared on the Dorsey Show he closed his eyes and pretended he was on stage with a lot of people cheering for him. He hunched his shoulders, swung his head from side to side, and jiggled his left leg harder than ever, putting everything he had into the number. The method worked. The Dorsey Show received more fan mail than it ever had before. "Heartbreak Hotel" became number one on *Billboard's* national survey of hits.

Elvis was so busy driving from place to place he could hardly notice. Also he was tired. After singing in Florida one night, he collapsed in bed with chills, a splitting headache, and nausea. In the morning he felt too weak to get up.

He was dimly aware that Scotty and Bill took him to a hospital, where he was put in a white gown and laid in a narrow white bed, and given medicine. In the back of his mind was a vague sense that something was wrong, but the coolness of the pillow caused him to close his eyes gratefully and sleep.

When he woke up the next day and realized where he was, he got out of bed and dressed hurriedly. He got in touch with Scotty and Bill. "Don't cancel tonight's show. I'm coming." He left the hospital even though his head pounded and his legs felt as though they were made of straw. Things were going too great for him to cancel out on anything. He was afraid that if he didn't show up, all his good fortune would vanish.

RCA wanted him to record a long-playing album of his most popular songs in New York City. Elvis thought this recording session would be easier because many of the songs he sang every week on tour: "Blue Suede Shoes," "Tutti Frutti," "Money Honey," "Blue Moon," "Just Because." He knew them as well as he knew his own name. Even so there were problems. The technicians complained that Elvis moved around so much they couldn't record his voice. They wanted him to stand still in front of the mike. But Elvis couldn't sing those hot, fast-paced songs standing still. Finally they figured out a way for him to play his guitar less so his voice would stand out more.

Elvis realized everyone expected him to decide when a song was going well enough to be recorded. He didn't feel comfortable about criticizing Scotty and Bill and D.J. though, so if he thought someone in the band was off-beat, he just kept suggesting they do it again until it sounded right. Eventually they did and there were no hard feelings.

They'd been through ten songs when Steve Sholes of RCA said, "Elvis, your fingers are sore and bleeding. Why don't you stop?"

Elvis looked at his fingers in surprise. "Well, it was going so good, I didn't want to break it up."

"One reason you're a success, you know, is that you're really willing to work."

"Thanks. That's one of the nicest things anyone's ever said about me."

The LP album was sent to the stores with a picture of Elvis tearing through a rock song. The record immediately went to the number eleven spot on national charts.

Colonel Parker called, "Elvis, Paramount Pictures wants to give you a screen test. Hal Wallis, the producer, saw you on the Dorsey Show. He also knows how you knocked 'em dead in person at the Paramount theaters.

Elvis still couldn't believe he had been asked

to go to Hollywood, even when he got there in April. A country boy like him — with no training? He thought of his heroes, Tony Curtis and James Dean. How could he ever be actors like them?

He went to a different kind of studio from radio and TV. Here there was no stage. The camera was smaller than the TV camera. A director was in charge. He told Elvis to put on jeans and a workshirt. He introduced him to another actor and placed them in front of some trees. "Now go through as many emotions as you can think of," he ordered.

Elvis blushed. He had no idea what he was doing but he started "acting" angry. He shouted and waved his arms. He poked the actor's chest. He stomped around puffing a cigar. He reminded himself that when he performed on stage, he "acted"; this was just a little bit different. He pretended the other actor was a friend and put his arm around him. After a while the director called it quits.

When Elvis saw himself on film, he cringed. He looked like a heavy, awkward blend of his mother and father. Depressed, he was sure he didn't have a chance to be in the movies. "We'll let you know" was all Hal Wallis said.

Elvis went to appear on the Milton Berle television program. Because of his television appearances, Parker was able to ask several thousand dollars for a live performance now. Elvis was earning much more money.

He bought a ranch house in Memphis for his folks. He added a swimming pool. Then, because Memphis teenagers swarmed around looking for him, he had a stone wall built. But even with spikes on top, it didn't keep people out. His cars were marked up with names written with lipstick or nail files. Porch furniture was stolen. Grass picked. Vernon and Gladys were very happy to be living in the first nice house of their lives, even though they had trouble getting out the driveway for all the cars that gathered on their street. They filled the house with albums of pictures and articles about their son.

Parker arranged for Elvis to appear at the Frontier Hotel in Las Vegas. Only rich people, mostly over fifty, could afford the cost of dinner and the performance in the fancy hotel. Not many people bought tickets. The ones who did come were not pleased by rock music or Elvis's style. His contract was cancelled. Elvis could see he was not a success with older people.

Parker concentrated on arranging more television appearances for him. In June there came another Milton Berle TV show. In July, it was Steve Allen's show. In September, it would be the Ed Sullivan show. Steve Allen turned him into a comic. He had to dress like a cowboy whose name was "Tumbleweed" and sing western songs. In another skit he was put in a tuxedo and told to sing "Hound Dog," without moving, while standing next to a real, droopy-looking hound dog. "Hound Dog" became an immediate best-selling record. *Time, Newsweek* and *Life* Magazines took notice.

The new fanfare brought letters from people who claimed to be the authors of the songs "Heartbreak Hotel," "Hound Dog," and "Don't Be Cruel," who wanted money. Elvis had to hire a lawyer to handle these claims. Some letters contained threats to his life. Women accused Elvis of fathering their children. Elvis was upset and scared when such letters came, but Parker told him that when you were a star, you were a target for all sorts of schemes.

Elvis pushed his fears in the background when he learned that Hal Wallis wanted to sign him up to do three full-length films. He was really going to be a movie actor!

14: The Movies

Elvis had the script for his first film memorized before he was scheduled to be in Hollywood, August, 1956.

The film was called *The Reno Brothers.* It was about two brothers who lived with their mother at the time of the Civil War. The older brother leaves his fiancée to fight in the war but Elvis, the younger brother, is too young to go. Word comes that the older brother dies in battle. When Elvis grows older, he marries the same girl his brother loved, not realizing they were ever engaged. The elder brother returns, however, which puts Elvis in a dilemma. The film ends with him dying from gunshot wounds. Elvis was worried how he'd do the love scene, but he looked forward to the death scene.

The producer of the film decided it was crazy not to have Elvis sing, so four songs were added to the film, and the title was changed to *Love Me Tender.* Elvis showed up eager for work every day, but the shooting schedule went slower than he expected. Also the story was not shot in sequence. Each scene took several "takes" until it was right, which was at least something Elvis was used to in recording sessions.

He practiced lassoing, coiling up a rope and tossing it at the steering wheel of a small truck about ten feet in front of him. He kept missing. A newspaper reporter and photographer approached him for an interview. He told them, "I got to practice being a cowboy." Reporters and photographers were everywhere he went, but in Hollywood they sought other stars, not just him.

"How do you like Hollywood?" the newspaperman asked.

"I've met the nicest people out here. Debra Paget is the most beautiful girl in the world." He looked around for his co-star and saw her sitting on a fence. He dropped the lasso and ran over to her, plopping in her lap. She squealed and protested. She was holding a calf by a rope. "Never a dull moment with you, Elvis," she said. She was always nice to him, he reflected. He was not so sure about the other movie people he met at the commissary, where everyone had lunch. Strangers either snubbed him or wanted him to make business deals.

While the film was being edited, Elvis went to Tupelo, Mississippi, his hometown, where on September 26th it had been declared Elvis Presley Day. On the fairgrounds where he had first sung "Old Shep" in the contest, he resang the song and gave a show. Twenty thousand

Elvis performs at the state fair in Tupelo

people, including all his relatives, were there. He was honored with a parade, a key to the city, and a cake in the shape of a guitar. The $10,000 he was to be paid for doing the show, he turned over to the town. He was given a tremendous homecoming.

From there he went to New York City for the first of three appearances on the Ed Sullivan television show. Sullivan ordered that Elvis be shown only above the waist on camera. "No viewer wants to see your vulgar leg jiggling," he said. Elvis was hurt but said nothing. A week after the show Ed Sullivan received hundreds of protesting letters. "Love Me Tender," the theme from the yet-to-be-released movie, became number one on the hit parade.

Elvis's blend of rock and blues created a whole new field of music. His style spread in waves around the world. Other singers imitated him. His haircut was copied. Guitars sold in huge quantities. In October his second LP was released with songs like "Ready Teddy," "Rip It Up," "Long Tall Sally," "Love Me." His records stayed in the top spot for months.

Wherever he went police had to protect him. He could no longer just go down to the drugstore. His friends gave him disguises to wear. He avoided restaurants, for if he went he would be besieged by autograph seekers, and then the owner would blame him for causing a disturbance. He had to be careful to avoid fights. Often he had to stay behind in a hotel room while his friends went out. When he got desperate for something to do, he'd rent a movie theatre or skating ring after closing hours.

Newspapers and magazines published stories about him. Headlines were: "Elvis Presley — He Can't Be, But He Is" ... "The Nation's Smash

Sensation"... "Rockin', Rollin', Wrigglin', Guitarin' Elvis Presley"... "America's Greatest New Talent of the Century." Elvis and his friends searched them out, amazed how often the stories contained wrong facts and misquotes. Elvis saw pictures of himself with women he was said to be marrying. One said he had only six months to live.

He didn't tell his parents about these articles. They made him too angry. But Colonel Parker said, "Cool it. It's part of success. The fact that they write about you is all that matters. If they didn't, you'd be nowhere. Just keep those reporters guessing. That's the secret."

Then worse attacks came. Someone nicknamed him "Elvis the Pelvis." Critics called his movements "repulsive" and his lyrics "gross." Parents were urged to lock up their children when he came to town. Ministers condemned him, linking him with rock n' roll, hot rods, and reefers. A disc jockey burned 600 of his records in a park. Elvis was blamed for juvenile delinquency. In the *Chicago Sun-Times* John Crosby wrote "his act borders on obscenity."

Elvis was very discouraged. "How can people be so intolerant?" he repeatedly asked his friends, who sought to reassure him. He tried to sing standing still, but he felt like a dog straining at a leash. He had no zest; worse, he didn't enjoy it. "I can't sing with a beat if I stand still." Music, he thought, was supposed to vibrate through his whole body like he learned in church. He sang with the voice and body God gave him.

He worried about the criticism as he prepared to give a concert at the Cotton Bowl in Dallas. He heard people had come two days ahead of time to camp in the ticket line. In his hotel outside the city, where he was supposed to be hidden, a mob of girls made a giant pyramid of their bodies to the window of his room. Elvis stood at the window and and waved to them. He threw out his handkerchief to great cheers and cries for attention. A girl knocked on the door, having managed to sneak by the hotel guards. Elvis talked to her. She showed him where she'd carved his name in her arm. He thought that was silly. Other girls were waiting in the lobby.

That night he was driven in a Cadillac to the stage set up in the middle of the field. A crowd of 26,000 was there and making more noise than at any football game. It was ecstatic pandemonium. Elvis thought, These people don't want me to stand still. If they didn't want to see me beat time with my legs, they would just listen to my records. He felt challenged to give them his best.

He sang for two hours. Happy about the deafening screams, at the end he sang "Hound Dog" and let himself rock off stage, all the while singing "You ain't nothin' but a hound dog/cryin' all the time" over and over again. He kneeled raunchily in the grass, rose, and kneeled again. The effect was electrifying.

"Oh Elvis, I'm going to die," someone shrieked. Some girls fainted. He finally edged himself over to the Cadillac, waiting to whisk him away into the dark night. He had as much fun as the crowd.

When the movie *Love Me Tender* was finally ready, it opened at 500 theaters across the country. Colonel Parker beamed and said, "That is five times as many theaters as the average film gets. Now we are upping the fee for a live show by you to $25,000 a night!"

With offices in Memphis and Hollywood, Colonel Parker was busy. He saw to it that the headquarters for the Elvis Presley Fan Club sent out word to its members of all Elvis's TV appearances and new records and urged them to write letters requesting more of Elvis. He'd hired nine secretaries to handle the 4,000 letters and phone calls Elvis received a day. He had also hired a company to market special Elvis Presley products, which earned millions of dollars a month. There were Elvis Presley socks, skirts, blouses, bracelets, handkerchiefs, sweaters, purses, pencils, bubble gum, jeans, games, sodas, pajamas, diaries, pictures, belts, ties, statues, book ends, guitars, lipsticks, cards, buttons, sneakers, photograph albums, combs, hairbrushes, hats, and perfume. Elvis read an article in *Look Magazine* about these products that stated: "Elvis Presley's fame is a legend of the American Dream of success that is overshadowed by a nightmare of bad taste." Elvis thought there were too many things, but he let Colonel Parker handle them. To Colonel Parker he'd become an industry, of which he earned twenty-five percent. To his friends he'd become an idol.

By the end of 1956 Elvis and Parker expected to earn about two million dollars. Although most of the money would be paid out in expenses and salaries, plus ninety percent to the U.S. government in taxes, Elvis received $500,000. He was floating sky-high. The money and acclaim were staggering. He knew his fans were the ones who made him such a success. He owed everything to them. He had been able to tell his father to quit his job at the factory. He had received five gold records from RCA, each one given to him after the sale of one million copies. The television shows. The movie stars. The thunderous applause. The clothes, the cars, the jewelry. Everything had come so quickly. Much more than he'd ever imagined.

15: Land of Grace

Elvis was stretched out on the couch of his cluttered Memphis house, talking with his parents. He'd recently come back from Hollywood, where he'd acted in his second movie, *Loving You*. In it he played an orphan who became a singer and sang seven songs. His parents had visited the set. The director had even put his mother in the last audience scene. "Mom," he said, his eyes glancing over the pile of teddy bears he'd been sent by fans and the pictures of him on the wall, "you've turned this place into a museum."

She laughed. "Well, that's what happens when you have a famous son. Colonel Parker says your success is like nothing this country has ever known. He says you are number one in more fields of music than anyone else."

"He's afraid the Army is trying to put an end to it all. I passed my physical, and they said I can expect to be drafted soon."

"Oh Elvis!"

"Well, it's a way of getting the rest you always wanted me to have. But I'll be with a bunch of men — and they haven't always been my greatest fans!" He laughed.

Vernon said, "You won't have any money worries unless you keep spending it like you do."

"Dad, I am glad you're keeping track." He sat up, rubbing his hands together. "I think we need a new place to live. Why Mom can't even hang out the laundry here without stirring up attention. You've changed the phone number a dozen times. I want a place to live where we can really be protected. Of course, rich folks won't think we belong near them."

Gladys said, "Are you going to fight being drafted?"

"I don't know. I'd sure like not to go, but then I'd probably get more bad write-ups."

Vernon said, "Maybe people need time to cool off. If you're gone, they won't have a target."

"Maybe they'll forget me too."

"There are your films for them to see."

"Yeah, at least they can be seen more than once. That's why I want to be a good actor."

"How long can all this last?" Gladys sighed.

"I don't know." Elvis stood up to go out. "I try not to think about it."

Soon Elvis was back in Hollywood for the third film, *Jailhouse Rock*. In this film he played the part of a man in jail whose cellmate teaches him how to play the guitar and to sing. Later when they're out of prison Elvis becomes famous and the former friend wants a share in Elvis' earnings.

He was glad to be back among other stars like himself. Hollywood was a place where he could wear his fanciest clothes without feeling conspicuous, because most of the others tried to outshine each other in dress too. Colonel Parker made him pose for an album cover in a solid gold lamé suit. He hated the outfit. It was too heavy and cumbersome.

After the filming he went to the studio to record the songs for the film. The first day he and the technical crew worked fifteen hours on the songs. Elvis felt good about the way they were going. The rhythm was lively, his voice responsive, a lot was done.

The second day he listened to tapes of songs he was to do along with the Jordonnaires. He had the lyrics memorized, but the musicians were not in sync with him. They worked on the numbers for about an hour. Then Elvis got bored. He and the band were not clicking. He called a break and went over to the piano, plunking out "Lord Take My Hand," a spiritual he'd learned when he was a boy. The four Jordonnaires came over and sang along with him.

Elvis began "Peace in the Valley" and loved it when the Jordonnaires harmonized with him. He did another and another.

At length one of the technicians said, "Hey Elvis, have you forgotten about us?"

"I'm warming up," Elvis said, shrugging tiredly. "Let's break for lunch."

All through lunch melodies of gospel songs ran through Elvis' head. He wanted to do more. When he returned to the studio, he went right back to the piano and plunked out "Swing Low, Sweet Chariot." The rest of the musicians took their places and restlessly shuffled their sheet music. "Come join me," Elvis said to the Jordonnaires.

"We can't."

"Why not?" Elvis turned around and looked at the band. "What's wrong?"

Someone said, "We're not going to listen to you doing spirituals when we have to cut these songs for the film."

Another added, "We want to finish and stop foolin' around."

Something in Elvis flared. All those days working out his style, all those grinding days on the road, all the times he'd sung even when he was wringing wet and exhausted, all those feelings welled up. To complain about the way he did things seemed unfair. The only reason they were there was because of him. They were getting their money, so why did they push him? He was going to get his job done the way he always did. He just couldn't sing on demand. He had to feel right about the music first. Scotty and Bill knew that. Besides, knocking spirituals rubbed him the wrong way. They were sacred. He stood up and angrily left the studio.

He put on his sunglasses, hopped in his Rolls

Royce and drove away. There'd be no songs recorded that day. Next time maybe they'd realize that he'd earned his right to run recording sessions to suit himself. On the road awhile he began to feel silly. The guys probably thought he'd acted too cocky. Maybe he was just upset about having to go in the Army and possibly losing everything.

The next day he went back to work but didn't say a word about the incident. Neither did the others. And, the recording got done.

When he got back to Memphis, he more than ever wanted a place to live where he could relax and do what he wanted. He bought a country mansion next to a church he'd seen on the road to Tupelo from Memphis. It was set far from the road in the middle of thirteen acres of land. It was big and majestic and peaceful. He named it "Graceland," because it was beautiful and because God's grace gave it to him.

Elvis had fun renovating the house with his mom's help. In the basement he put a game room with a pool table and all his gold records on the wall. Near that was a projection room so he could watch movies whenever he wanted. His room he had painted dark blue with one entire wall of mirrors. On the entrance hall ceiling he had clouds painted with blinking lights for stars at night. In the living room he ordered the walls painted purple with gold trim and hung white drapes.

New Rolls Royce in front of Graceland mansion in Memphis, Tennessee

Surrounding the thirteen acres was a ten-foot metal fence, which two of his uncles guarded. Wrought on the gates was an iron figure of Elvis playing his guitar. Elvis's Aunt Delta and grandmother came to live at Graceland with him and his parents. That way he stayed close to his folks. He loved how impressed they were with Graceland.

Then came the dreaded letter that instructed

him to report to his Army draft board on January 20th, 1958. Elvis's stomach heaved at the prospect. Colonel Parker exploded, "Why, you have a contract for your next film. Paramount has already started filming it. We'll have to get a deferment."

Elvis won a two month reprieve. He decided to go in just like other American men and not claim any special treatment. More than anything he didn't want to act better than anyone else. But Parker said not to let the Army put him in the entertainment department where he'd have to perform for free either.

Elvis went out to Hollywood and acted in *King Creole*. It had eleven songs and was about a singer in New Orleans who gets involved with hoodlums. Elvis worked harder on it than ever, because he was afraid it would be his last. The director told him he'd done his finest acting.

Elvis didn't have many free days left. He went back to Memphis and had a visit with Scotty and Bill. He had the feeling that everything would be different when he got out of the army despite Colonel Parker's assurances. As though to make the fun last as long as he could, on his last night home he threw a party for everyone he knew.

16: The Crunch

Elvis left Graceland at 6 A.M. In his car were his parents, a friend named Judy, and Colonel Parker. Other friends and cousins followed. When he arrived at the Army office, dozens of photographers and reporters converged upon him, snapping pictures and asking questions. Elvis joked with them as they followed him in with the other recruits to have their physical examinations. He felt silly causing such a furor and knew that what they really wanted was to see his hair get shaved, which irritated him. The Colonel handed out balloons, turning Elvis's entry into the Army into a grand publicity event.

Elvis, along with the other men his age, was sworn in by an Army officer and then sent to the doctor. The photographers and reporters went right in with him. After the doctor checked him over, he had to go to the barber. Everyone crowded around to watch. The barber had a crew cut so short it made his ears stick out like flaps, so Elvis was sure none of his hair would be spared. He sat in the chair with a smock around his neck and watched the barber get out the clippers.

"Hey, Elvis," came a voice from the crowd, "how do you feel about getting shorn?" Elvis shook his head.

The barber started clipping his neck. When the hairs fell, people scooped them up. The barber remarked, "You have the most valuable hair in history."

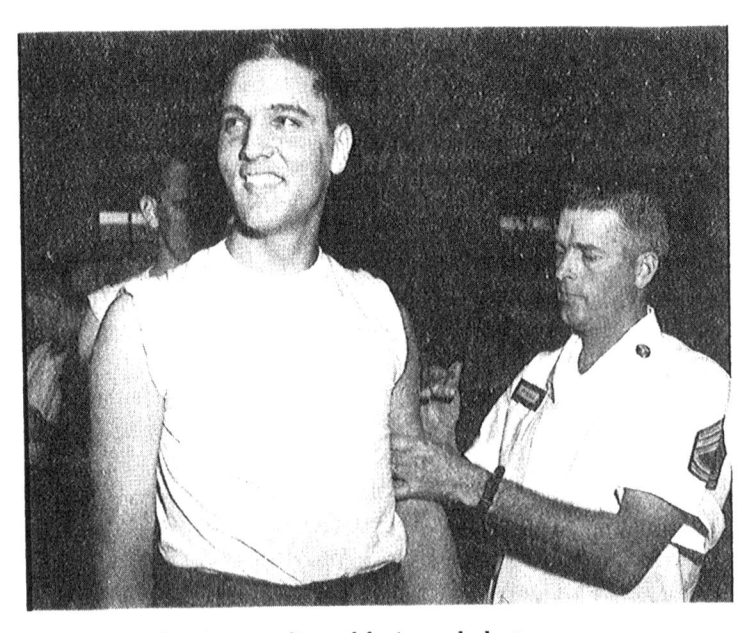

Entering the Army: clipped hair and shots

In no time Elvis's hair was no longer than an inch all around. Embarrassed, he said, "It looks like a lawn mower just ran over me." He rubbed the top of his head. "I feel cold."

Everyone laughed.

From there he was ordered to dress in a khaki army uniform. As he changed, leaving behind his own clothes, he realized that no longer was he boss of his own life. From now on he'd have to obey Army rules. He wasn't at all sure he was going to like this experience, no matter how much he claimed he wanted to be treated like everyone else. He wished he could go back to Graceland.

But, no, it was time to say goodbye to his parents and friends and board a bus that was going to take him to Fort Chaffee, Arkansas. As the dingy, crowded bus took off, Elvis waved a last time to his family, who would return to Graceland in his Cadillac. He sat back sullenly next to another young man equally somber. He felt torn from all that was familiar.

On the way the men were let out at a coffee shop to eat. As Elvis was served some spaghetti, an argument broke out between the waitresses over who would get his place and chair. Before he finished eating, a crowd of girls burst in the restaurant and quickly spotted Elvis. They crowded around him, talking and requesting his autograph. The other guys eyed him strangely, but Elvis felt happier.

Back in the bus the guy next to him said, "Is it always like that?"

"Yep. I guess I'll worry when it's not."

Waiting in Fort Chaffee were about three hundred more girls, and photographers, and reporters determined to keep the rest of the country informed about Elvis's induction. They followed him even to Fort Hood in Texas, where Elvis was to get "basic training" in the Armored Division. Finally the newspapermen were ordered off-base and Elvis settled down to a routine of early to bed, early to rise, classroom instruction, shooting practice, and endurance tests on an outdoors obstacle course.

Elvis knew that the other fellows were watching him because he was a celebrity and he didn't want to make any enemies. At meals and at bedtime someone was sure to make remarks like "Miss your teddy bears?" or "I bet you'd rather jiggle than march." The sergeant attacked him one morning for not getting dressed early enough: "Maybe you need some rock n' roll to wake up, rather than reveille?" Elvis noticed that if he complained, the guys took offense, but if they griped about something, everyone took it lightly. He knew the newspapermen, too, were watching closely as he tried to get along as well as he could, but he couldn't relax.

He found out that the Army permitted soldiers to live off base if they had parents to support, so Elvis applied for permission. It was granted. In his spare time he found a house in Killeen to rent. Once his parents got there Elvis felt more at ease. With them he could talk about his new albums released by RCA, wear his favorite clothes, and see the premiere of his film, *King Creole*.

But his mother didn't seem to be well. She spent long hours napping and ate very little. Her skin looked pale, even yellowish. Finally he and his father decided she should go back to Memphis and see the doctor. Elvis drove his parents to the train and said, "Be sure to let me know right away what's the matter." He hugged his mother extra long.

"Don't worry. I'm sure it's nothin' but a bug."

The next day Vernon telephoned to say the doctor wanted her to go into the hospital for tests.

Two days later he called and said she had a liver infection. "Your mother won't like it, but the doctor thinks you'd better come home."

Elvis' heart suddenly fluttered. "It's not serious?" he asked, knowing it must be.

"The doctor can't find out the cause." Vernon sounded tense.

Elvis hung up the phone and raced for his sergeant's office. "Sir, I have to go home. My mother's sick." He almost choked on the words.

"Emergency leave, Presley? I'll have to see about it."

Elvis spent a night tormented with fear for his mother's life. The next morning when he was in the kitchen peeling potatoes, an aide informed him that he could go.

In a state of numbed panic Elvis put on a clean uniform and went to the airport to catch the next airplane out. He had to wait three hours. He tried a cup of coffee but it nauseated him.

He finally got to Memphis and then to the hospital by 9:15 P.M. shortly before evening visiting hours were to end.

She lay propped up between the white sheets, her dark hair damp from the hot August weather. He leaned over her, kissed her cheek, and smelled medicine. Just being able to see her made him feel somewhat relieved.

Her hands held him weakly. "Oh, Elvis, you shouldn't have come."

Vernon rose from his seat at the side of the bed and put his arm around Elvis. "Son, I'm glad you made it."

"Mom, you just got to get better." He held her hand.

"I am, don't worry. My, but you look handsome in that uniform. Wait'll your cousins see you."

"Good and proper, eh?" he teased, wanting to make her smile.

"I want to go home," she said with a sigh.

Vernon said, "I've been spending the night here so she would have somebody close. You know, none of us knew how sick she was. She put up a good front and didn't tell us. The doctor says this is the best hospital around and she is strong, so she should get well."

"Let me stay tonight, Dad. I'd like to."

After the curfew Elvis talked to his mom until she grew sleepy. He stretched out on a cot in the room but didn't sleep much.

In the morning Vernon returned, along with five of Elvis's friends. Elvis went back to Graceland with them. Seeing Graceland made him sadder than ever. He had wanted her to enjoy it. It had no appeal to him when she was in the hospital. He went to his room and slept awhile.

When he went back in the afternoon, he tried to interest her in a card game. He bought her a Coke. But she seemed limp. Elvis hated to see her suffering. The doctor came and made him wait in another room. Elvis was so dejected he couldn't talk to his friends when they came to visit too. He prayed that she would get well. He'd do anything, he promised.

That night Vernon said he would stay over, so at the end of visiting hours Elvis reluctantly kissed Gladys goodbye, promising to be there in the morning. He went home but couldn't sleep.

The phone rang. Elvis answered it in the dark. His dad was crying. "She passed on, Elvis, just now, a few minutes ago." A pain stabbed Elvis. The worst had happened. He couldn't believe it.

The one person in all the world who'd been warm and loving as the sunshine to him. She was still so young — only forty-two. It wasn't right. Grief and rage mixed and he moaned, "Oh God!" He buried his face in his pillow and was shaken by sobs.

By the time of the funeral Elvis was hardly aware that several thousand fans lined the street to the church. Many more sent condolences. Four hundred friends and relatives sat in the church and listened to the eulogy and the Blackwood Brothers singing his mama's favorite song, "Memories." The strains of the music brought tears to many a cheek besides Elvis's and Vernon's. From the church they proceeded to the cemetery where her grave was marked with a life-size marble sculpture of Jesus flanked by two angels.

His mother had been the center of their lives, and now just he and his father were left.

Elvis returned to his Army duties, resigned to doing what was expected of him, no matter what. In September he was sent to Europe via New York City, where hordes of girls lined up to see him off. A band played "Hound Dog" and "All Shook Up." Elvis pretended to be delighted but he really didn't care. His heart was buried with his mother.

17: Germany

Knowing about Elvis's loss, the guys on the ship to Germany were more friendly. When the boat landed on October 1st in Bremerhaven, about five hundred fans welcomed Elvis. He was glad to meet Europeans who liked his music, but he was rushed to a train that bore him to Friedberg, a town in central Germany. At that post reporters from different countries were allowed to watch Elvis for three days, after which they were barred.

Elvis learned his assignment was to be a scout jeep driver for Sgt. Ira Jones. According to Army theory, if an enemy attacked, the armored tank men depended on the jeep drivers to scout ahead and check the roads, drawing maps and looking out for enemy weapons. In 1958 the United States was not involved in any warfare, but the Army organized long practice sessions, called maneuvers, just in case. For his part Elvis would get paid $135 a month.

Most of the guys lived in barracks on the Army post, but Elvis arranged for his father and grandmother Minnie to come over so he could live with them. He even paid the way for a couple of his Memphis buddies to visit. First they stayed in a large resort hotel in Bad Homburg, famous for its healing baths. On leave he and his friends exercised, swam, and rode horseback. They ate huge, delicious meals and roughhoused in their rooms, just like they did at home. It was easy to fool around, because most of the day he didn't have much to do and got restless. It was hard not to have to sing nor learn lines for a new show or recording.

He bought a BMW and paid an outrageous rent for a white stucco two-story house. There was a picket fence around the house, but it didn't look as if they were going to be bothered by huge numbers of fans. The mail brought five hundred to a thousand letters a day, plus boxes of candy and cookies, which Elvis shared with the guys in his unit. Vernon hired two secretaries to take care of the mail.

Day after day Elvis got up at 5 A.M. to dress, eat breakfast, and drive to the post by 7 A.M. There he'd report to Sergeant Jones and start driving around or cleaning up the office. At least on the road he saw some countryside, very different from America, with chimney sweeps and kids playing soccer. With a lot of time to fill he went with some of his new friends to work out in karate. Karate appealed to him because it was physically tough but also demanded much body finesse. He though he could use it to protect himself in public. He got very skilled at it.

Nineteen fifty-nine passed slowly. The memory of his mother and the way things used to be lingered in his mind. Colonel Parker was doing what he could back in the States to keep Elvis from being forgotten. RCA made albums out of songs Elvis had recorded but never before sold. These were best-sellers but after a while, for the first time in three years, Elvis did not have a number one song. Colonel Parker decided to prepare a calendar for 1960 with Elvis's discharge date circled, four color pictures of Elvis in the Army, and a "personal message" from Elvis in Germany.

When Elvis's time in the Army was "getting short," his assignments became more difficult. His unit was sent out one day in a forested wilderness during the coldest part of winter. The men were to have a mock combat with another unit. The other unit's officer had promised his men fifty dollars and a three-day pass if they could capture Elvis. For several days the tanks rolled back and forth in the hills, avoiding each other. Then when Elvis was out studying a road, a G.I. in a jeep drove up, jumped out, and took him prisoner by surprise. Elvis gave in, but soon after his unit's tanks rolled up the road and took the G.I. prisoner.

His friend, Charlie said, "We knew they'd try

to take you, so we kept an extra special watch on you." Elvis thought it was a great joke.

He decided to have the guys to his house for a party. Joe Esposito, a friend from Chicago, asked him if he would like a date with the daughter of an Air Force captain. "Sure, bring her along," Elvis said.

The night of the party Elvis had lots of food and records to play. Room was made for dancing. Joe brought his date and the girl for Elvis. Her name was Priscilla Beaulieu. She had a pretty, sweet face with long, curly brown hair. He was a bit shocked to learn that she was only sixteen. Although she was short, she acted older.

After they'd talked awhile, she said, "My father was against my coming here, but my mother was for it. That's funny because when she first heard of you, she said she wouldn't cross the street to meet you."

"Yeah, I know, I'm the product of immoral, degenerate capitalism."

She laughed and asked him about Memphis. Elvis found it easy to tell her about Graceland. She told him how she had been an orphan and wanted to go back to America. Being with her was like being with his high school friends before he'd become famous.

They were interrupted by other people arriving at the party who wanted to talk with Elvis. Priscilla didn't mind. Like Elvis, she didn't drink or smoke. Elvis danced with her, and so did others. After a few hours she said, "Daddy said I have to be home by twelve. He's afraid your being a star will be bad for me."

"He's absolutely right, but will you see if you can come over for dinner next Friday?" She agreed.

Friday he sent his father to pick her up. Then he, Priscilla, Vernon, and Minnie ate southern fried chicken, mashed potatoes, and succotash made by his grandmother. Afterwards Vernon left to go out on a date with Dee, a woman he'd met in Germany. Minnie turned on television and watched a German variety show.

Priscilla and Elvis drank coffee at the table. Elvis said, "My dad's found a gal from Alabama here. It's been hardly more than a year since my mother died."

"You must feel bad."

"It's hard to get used to someone else. I don't like to think about it."

"Maybe she helps him get over her."

"I suppose so." Elvis stood up and led Priscilla into the living room, where they sat down and watched TV with Minnie. He put his arm around Priscilla and kidded around with her. She was shy and natural. He wanted to get her a present.

The word came finally. The Army was to send him home in March. One part of him whooped for joy, another part was bothered by having to leave Priscilla. Colonel Parker wrote that Hal Wallis, the producer of Paramount Pictures was already shooting scenes for his next movie. Parker joked that he'd scared Wallis to death by telling him that Elvis was planning to reinlist. On the other hand, no record of Elvis had been on the charts for five months. He had to catch up!

So Elvis finished his Army duties, filled out the required forms, and gathered his stuff, needing twenty duffel bags just for his mail.

Vernon and Priscilla saw him off at the airport. Priscilla wore the diamond wristwatch he had given her. She said, "I wish I could see you in the States."

"We'll get together somehow, honey," he said, patting her arm. He was wearing his dress uniform with the brimmed cap and thinking it wouldn't be too long before he wouldn't have the uniform anymore.

"Be sure to write."

"I'll call you. I hate letter-writing." He put his arms around her and kissed her. Then he said goodbye to his father and boarded the plane with the others.

Charlie, Joe, and the rest of the guys were already in high spirits. Going home to pick up the pieces where they'd left off had put them in an hilarious mood.

The plane landed in New Jersey. Before Elvis

got down the ramp newsmen bombarded him with questions: "Was he glad to be home? What did he think of the Army? How did he like European women? What were his plans?" No one asked him about his music.

From there he got on a train to Memphis and was amazed that at every station along the way crowds of people waved and welcomed him. In Memphis a policeman took him in his squad car through thronged streets. Elvis waved, touched to see so many people still thought of him. He wanted to stop and talk with them but the policeman drove right through until he was well inside the Graceland gates.

After eighteen months Graceland looked more magnificent than ever. "I'm a free man at last," he shouted and celebrated with his family and friends.

Being back was glorious. He went to Nashville to record new songs for an album RCA planned to call *Elvis Is Back*. Before Elvis opened his mouth RCA already had a million orders for the album. He went to Miami to tape a TV program with Frank Sinatra and was mobbed with fans and reporters. Then Elvis went to Hollywood and dressed in an elegant black formal suit and black suede shoes appeared at a press conference. With him were an entourage of friends who were hired to assist him with his wardrobe, cars, and travel plans. He was ready to go, man, go.

18: Disillusioned Movie Actor

Elvis stayed in Hollywood to make the film, *G.I. Joe*. He went home to Graceland for a while and found it empty and lonely. His father had married Dee and moved out of Graceland to live with her and her three sons in a house in back. Elvis missed his mother more than ever, often dreaming about her. Now that he had two number one records — "It's Now or Never" and "Are You Lonesome Tonight?" — he wanted to share his success with her, but he could not.

So, he went back to Hollywood, taking his friends along with him for support. Colonel Parker considered making movies more profitable than live performances and got Elvis some big contracts. That was fine with Elvis for he wanted to be known for his acting as well as his singing.

When *G.I. Joe* was shown in theaters, a critic wrote that he was much "subdued and changed since he returned from military service." Another called him "wholesome" with "honey in his veins instead of blood." It was true in the film he sang without keeping time with his body unless given a special dance to do. Elvis wasn't as sure as the Colonel that this was a good sign.

Colonel Parker said, "Never you mind. The film is earning a fortune. And you appeal to more people than ever. Besides, remember how the critics wanted you to tone down. Now's your chance."

Elvis made another film, *Flaming Star*, in which he played a half-Indian. Then another, *Wild in the Country*, in which he was a poor boy accused of murder.

He rented a huge house and invited his friends — stars, singers, musicians, karate experts — to make use of it. So, if there wasn't a party going on, there were always the guys and girl friends visiting, playing games, or watching movies. Elvis had thousands of records in his collection. He felt free to go off in his rooms upstairs by himself if he wanted to, which were off-limits to his gang. He liked having people around him and things going on all the time. That way he didn't get bored, especially when he couldn't go out in public without being mobbed. He kept his own friendly mob close by. And his friends didn't criticize him the way strangers sometimes did.

He loved spending money, especially buying his friends things they could never afford, like Cadillacs and diamond wristwatches. One time he bought a dozen motorcycles so he and his friends could ride together. He loved to see the look on a guy's face when he handed him the keys to a white Eldorado and said, "It's all yours, man." The guys often borrowed money from him too, and he didn't mind if they didn't pay him back, which was most of the time. His father minded, but after all, Elvis figured, it was his money.

At Christmas time he sent for Priscilla, who was still in Germany, to spend the holidays with him in Memphis. With her there, the place seemed more like home. She was even more beautiful than he remembered. One night he said to her as they were cuddling on the couch, "Gee, it's nice having you here. Wish you didn't have to go back."

"I bet I could stay if I could get my parents to let me go to school here. They want me in an American school."

"You could live with Vernon and Dee while I'm in Hollywood and do whatever you want."

"Elvis, I'd love it!" Excitedly she jumped up. "Let's call them right now."

At first they said "no." Then Elvis got on the phone and explained how Priscilla could live a normal life with his dad's family. They finally agreed. Priscilla was enrolled in the Catholic High School for her senior year. When Elvis went back to Hollywood he liked thinking of her back home waiting for him.

He didn't see Scotty Moore or work with him anymore. Bill Black died of a brain tumor.

In the next year he made *Blue Hawaii, Follow That Dream*, and *Kid Galahad*. For kicks he bought a Cadillac limousine and had the body sprayed with a paint made of crushed diamonds and oriental fish scales. The trim was plated in gold. Some of his gold records were inset in the interior roof and gold lamé drapes covered the rear window. He put in a gold telephone, a gold razor and hair clippers, an intercom, a gold-plated TV, a phonograph, and a refrigerator that made ice cubes in two minutes. He used this to send for his dates, usually the actresses he worked with.

Another year was spent filming *Girls! Girls! Girls!, It Happened at the World's Fair*, and *Fun in Acapulco*. His acting wasn't getting any better because he wasn't getting any challenging parts. He was playing the same kind of handsome hero in every film with only a change in location. None of the films were shot in order of the story, so he felt out of touch with the dramatic build-up.

Elvis began to grow restless. He looked to his friends for fun. One time they dropped cherry bombs in the dressing rooms. Another time they chased each other around the set squirting water pistols. Or, they'd dress up in costumes and act silly.

"You'll get more serious scripts," the Colonel

promised, but then signed Elvis up for four more of the same old kind: *Kissin' Cousins, Viva Las Vegas, Roustabout,* and *Girl Happy.* Elvis called Priscilla but that didn't make him feel better. She was far away.

Well after midnight one night he went into the game room of his house to play pool. There were several guys and women hanging around, eating sandwiches. He lost a game to Ed. He turned on the television set to see what movie was on. The set remained dark, a tube blown. Elvis cracked his pool stick over the top, muttering to himself. Nothing was working right for him. The others were watching him. Sometimes he hated it when they waited for him to react, to see what his mood was. He felt like telling them all to leave but didn't. He snapped his knees.

"What's wrong, Elvis?" asked George, holding a Coke toward him. Elvis ignored him.

"Can I get you something?" asked fat Lamar.

"Forget it."

"Want some company?" asked a pretty woman.

"No," said Elvis. He went up to his room. He didn't like it there either. He wanted to go out. I'm a prisoner, he thought. "I can't go anywhere. My friends don't understand me, and I'm a lousy actor.

He looked at himself in the mirror. His blue silk shirt with the puffed sleeves seemed to sag.

He combed his hair back and spotted several gray hairs. Maybe, he thought, I will have white hair early like Dad. He decided to have it dyed. Not only that, but he would go on a yogurt and soup diet. He hated looking heavier on film than he did in the mirror. Maybe if he got very thin he would look better as an actor. Then there were his eyes: nearsighted, needing glasses when he wasn't in front of the camera.

He could go to bed, but he knew he would just toss and turn. What could he do? He didn't feel like driving around. His eyes fell on a motorized model airplane a friend had sent him. Maybe he'd fiddle with that for a while.

When the filming of boring *Tickle Me* was over, Elvis let off steam by buying a load of flashbulbs and floating them in the pool. He and the boys shot at them, relishing the explosions of light.

Then the Colonel signed him up for a movie, *Harum Scarum,* that was to be made in two and one-half weeks, so that there would be fewer expenses and therefore more profits.

All morning the crew worked outdoors. Director, cameraman, aides, and actors milled around performing their jobs. "Take one, scene twenty" clapped the board at intervals. Everyone was quiet, even those visitors and photographers permitted to visit. At noon they broke for lunch.

Except Elvis. To the band he said, "We'd better rehearse. The songs don't feel right and now is the only time we have to practice. Okay, fellas?"

They agreed and took their places where they would be filmed in the afternoon. With script in hand, Elvis and the band started off together. His words sounded flat, as if he were reading them for the first time. "We got to get this thing cookin'," he said anxiously. After forty-five minutes of vocalizing five songs, perspiration drenched his forehead, chest, and shirt. Elvis was angry. The songs sounded poor, and the band made mistakes in every line. In ten minutes they would be called to perform in front of the camera. His stomach signalled hunger. There was no time to eat, rest, or rehearse.

Elvis stormed over to Colonel Parker's office in the studio.

"Hi, boy," said the Colonel, rising from behind his immense desk with the row of elephant statues on top. Nearby was a bubble gum machine, a stuffed snowman, and a neon light display of Elvis's name.

"Colonel, this has gone too far! In five minutes the cameras are going to roll and no one's ready. I feel like calling in sick or quitting." Elvis's eyes smouldered, his lips pouted.

"Have you had lunch?" Elvis shook his head.

Disillusioned Movie Actor

"Well, let me get you a bite while we talk. They can wait." They walked through a room that was covered wall-to-wall with photos of Elvis and posters from his movies and another room covered with autographed pictures of celebrities. In the kitchen the Colonel got out bread and peanut butter and bananas for Elvis.

Elvis complained, "I can't work this way. In *Kissin' Cousins* I recorded nine songs in eight hours. They're all lousy."

"Elvis, with each film you make we get a best-selling album out of it."

Elvis squirmed uncomfortably. He wished he could find the words to convince the Colonel that something was missing, something he wanted badly. "No one takes me seriously. I want to be recognized as an actor. I want a script that allows me to do more than walk through scenes with a guitar close by."

"Your films have to be musicals. I try to get you the best deals. I figure the writers and directors know more about the scripts." They ate their sandwiches in tense silence.

Elvis resumed hotly, "That guy in the *Times* said *Tickle Me* was the silliest, feeblest, and dullest vehicle for me yet. I think he's right. I'm going to lose my audience if things don't get better. I'm thirty years old now. I feel dead." He brushed at the hair that fell over his dark eyes.

"Things are going great," said the Colonel, lighting a cigar. "Your voice is as golden as ever."

"I haven't had a number one hit in three years."

"Maybe you have a case of the jitters. You and I have been together for ten years and I want you to be happy. Look at the facts, boy. The films and albums earn you about six million dollars a year. You are the highest-paid entertainer the world has ever known. What more do you want?"

Elvis pushed himself away from the table. Back on the set he knew they would be impatient for him, yelling at the crew to do everything faster, faster. Did he really want to go along with them? He knew he made more pictures per year than other stars, but he wanted to be rewarded for his hard work, not just in dollars.

The Colonel rose and walked with him to the door. "We have the usual campaign planned for this picture: buttons, streamers, kits for the fan clubs, and some surprises." He chuckled.

"Okay, you win—for now," Elvis said, pretending to jab him in the ribs with a gun. Then he hurried back to the set.

19: Marriage and Other Changes

Elvis was at Graceland for a rest. He rolled over in his king-size bed and looked at the clock. Three P.M. Even though he'd gone to sleep around six A.M., this was late for him. He was glad to be home and away from the phoniness of Hollywood, where after making twenty-five films he'd begun to feel like a caricature of himself.

He got up and dressed. Looking out the window, he saw that it was a sunny spring afternoon. Clusters of tulips and daffodils that Priscilla had planted were at their peak. He trotted down the stairs and found his Aunt Delta, who made him a huge Spanish omelette.

He was eager to get outside, and as soon as he stepped out the front door and under an archway of stately trees with tiny leaves as yet unfurled, he sighed. Graceland lives up to its name, he thought, meandering down to the front gates where a crowd of about a hundred people gathered as usual. Some had spotted him and waved, calling his name. Elvis grinned back and greeted his uncle, who parted the great iron gates.

"Oh-h-h Elvis," a woman called, "you look so good."

"Thanks, ma'am." He signed her piece of paper.

"You sure were great in *Blue Hawaii*," a thin man said. "What's it like there?"

"Nothin' but beaches," said Elvis, continuing to sign photos and other souvenirs thrust at him.

"Where's your motorcycle?" asked a teenager.

"Restin'. I got me a go-cart now. It looks like a snowmobile on wheels. I race around here." He gestured toward the broad tree-lined paths, slightly laughing at himself. "Sure nice of you folks to come by."

"Oh Elvis, we wouldn't miss you for the world."

"Are you ever goin' to sing again?" a man shouted.

Elvis looked startled. Sing again? "You mean on stage?" Apparently the fan didn't count what he did in the movies as singing. Surely some changes had to be made or he'd lose all his fans.

He turned to talk to other fans, enjoying their interest. While they rapped as if old friends, cars passing by on the boulevard began stopping as more and more people recognized him. Pretty soon a commotion broke out at the shopping center that had opened up across the street.

Marriage and Other Changes 141

"Gotta go now," Elvis said regretfully. "See you later." The gates were securely fastened behind him.

On his way back to the house he stopped at the offices where the secretaries answered fan mail and his father managed business matters. He chatted with everyone and signed thousand-dollar checks to be given to the Boy Scouts, Goodwill, Salvation Army, Muscular Dystrophy Fund, and schools for orphans and retarded children. Then he went to the kennel to see his dogs, peacocks, monkey, and other pets.

Priscilla drove in. He went out to meet her. She was dressed in a black leotard and skirt. Her black hair was tied back with a yellow bandana. She kissed him and did a little pirouette in front of him. "Still doin' that high falutin' dancing?" he teased. "Come on, let's go riding at the ranch today."

"A dreamy idea. I'll be ready in a minute." She dashed into the house.

Joe Esposito and Alan Fortas, friends who also worked for him, waited inside. "Get the car ready," said Elvis with a cowboy drawl. "We're headin' for the Circle G Ranch."

Soon the four of them were zipping down the highway to Elvis's new ranch five miles over the Mississippi border. As they approached the fenced-in pasture of grazing cows and horses, Elvis said, "I hope the neighbors appreciate us."

They settled their things in the ranch house and headed for the corral. "I'll ride the first horse that comes to me," Elvis said. "Come here, pinto." A hired hand stood by laughing and waiting with halters and lead ropes.

Finally four horses were saddled. Alan and Joe sat aloft, gingerly holding onto the reins. Priscilla, sitting well on a palomino, laughed and said, "I don't think you guys know what you're doing."

"Just bounce," Elvis said kicking his horse. The horse jerked forward, throwing Elvis back in his seat. "Not exactly like that," he cracked, eyeing his horse's ears suspiciously.

They headed for the open acres of land under a canopy of clouds. The horses picked their way among the stones and bushes. Elvis and Priscilla hung back together. "You really look good on a horse," Elvis said, thinking how much the finishing school had done for her.

She smiled, then added hesitatingly, "Elvis, I have something serious to talk to you about. I'm twenty-one now, you know. I can't live at your house forever. People are beginning to talk. I can't do it any longer. My parents are asking questions."

"Aw, I don't want you to go."

"I don't want to either, baby."

He thought how much a part of the family she'd become. He knew his mother would have liked her. "Maybe we should, uh, get married?"

She looked at him gleefully. "Oh, Elvis, I'd always hoped you loved me enough to want to marry me." She turned serious. "But I don't know, maybe marriage will be different."

"At thirty-two years I ought to be ready for it." To himself he wondered if he really was. He'd always expected to have a family someday, but somehow he couldn't imagine himself a father. What would happen to his image? Would his fans like him married? These questions bothered him; still he felt ready to make a change. His life was in a rut.

That night they talked to Colonel Parker, who promised to organize a wedding with the greatest secrecy and protection against mob scenes. Priscilla decided to design her own dress.

Graceland was in a flurry, for the wedding was to take place in Las Vegas on May 1, 1967, just three weeks away. Everything had to be done without newspaper reporters catching on.

At midnight on April 31st, Priscilla and Elvis flew in a private plane to Las Vegas. Priscilla's parents and Vernon and Dee were already at the Aladdin Hotel where the wedding was to be. Colonel Parker sent Elvis and Priscilla in a limousine to get their marriage license at the courthouse. Then feeling giddy, as though they were playing a hoax on the world, they went to their hotel rooms to dress.

Elvis put on fancy black tuxedo pants, a velvet-brocaded vest and jacket, a bow tie, and put a white carnation in his lapel. Nervously he went down to the suite of the hotel owner, where the Nevada Supreme Court Judge waited with his Bible in hand, along with Colonel Parker, Priscilla's parents, Vernon and Dee, and Joe Esposito and high school buddy Marty Lacker, who were to be the best men, and their wives. Seeing the small formal group, Elvis knew a lot of other people were going to be upset at not being invited.

At 10 A.M. Priscilla came in with her sister. Her long, white, pearl-studded chiffon gown billowed around her. A crown set on the top of her black hair held the veil, which fell in a train down her back. She held a bouquet of pink rosebuds and a white Bible in one hand and with the other took Elvis's. Elvis whispered, "You look like a fairy queen." She smiled radiantly and said, "I can't believe this is really happening."

They faced the Judge in a corner of the room decked with white lilies, gladioli, and carnations. Elvis tried to stay serious through the solemn ritual and final exchange of gold rings and a kiss.

Then amidst congratulations they went to the ballroom where one hundred friends swirled noisily around them. The celebration continued all morning. There was a breakfast of ham and eggs, southern fried chicken, roast pig, salmon, oysters, and champagne. Violinists circulated playing "Love Me Tender" and other ballads. Photographers snapped them cutting their six-tiered wedding cake. Eventually they left the party to go to the new circular house that Elvis leased in Palm Springs, California.

About two months later, Priscilla said to him one night. "Elvis, I'm pregnant."

He looked at her surprised, then grinned. "Really, baby doll?"

She ran her hand over his hair. "You a father!" she giggled. He gave her a playful punch.

He couldn't resist telling the news to everyone he saw on the set, where he was working on a new film called *Speedway*. He had to finish still another film, *Stay Away Joe*, before he could go home to Memphis, where he wanted Priscilla to have the baby. By that time she was in her last two months.

It was February 1, 1968, when Priscilla said she was ready to go to the hospital. In his anxiety Elvis ordered his friends to follow him there in a second car just in case his car broke down. At the hospital Priscilla was led away by a nurse and he was made to wait. His friends and father kept him company.

Eight long hours later the nurse came for him. She took him down the hall and pointed out a tiny, dark-haired infant girl bundled up in a cradle. As he stared at her, feelings of love and longing tugged at his heart. Rather buoyantly he went to Priscilla's room and gave her a fierce hug. She looked tired, but smiling. "It was a lot harder than I expected," Priscilla said, "but how do you like Lisa Marie? Isn't she a doll?"

"I'll say," he said proudly and went off to show her off to his friends.

By the time Priscilla came home with Lisa Marie, thousands of cards, dolls, knitted booties, and blankets had been sent from fans.

Three weeks later Elvis went back to Hollywood for *Live a Little, Love a Little*. Priscilla was angry at him for leaving so soon. He didn't blame her, for he really didn't want to go. But he didn't want to break his contract, either.

When the film was done he came home and was amazed at how Lisa Marie had learned to sit up by herself. She looked more like him now with her square face, high forehead, and puckered mouth. He like to make her laugh. Priscilla said that Vernon spoiled her.

Elvis took Priscilla and Lisa Marie to Hawaii for a vacation. He also paid for some of his friends and their wives to go along. One night Priscilla complained. "Honey, I want to go away alone with you sometime. Just us."

"I hardly ever see the guys anymore. I thought they'd like a treat." He didn't understand what was bothering her, but he took her to California with him when he made his next film *The Trouble with Girls*. She spent most of her time with Lisa and visiting with friends.

Marriage and Other Changes   147

Now that he was a normal husband and father Elvis felt more confident, but he also noticed that when he walked down the street, people weren't stopping to stare at him. He was certain people had forgotten him and went to Colonel Parker demanding, "The next script I do must have no singing, all acting. No more silly roles. Also, I want to go back onstage."

Parker got him the script *Charro*. In it he wore dirty leather pants and appeared unshaven throughout. He didn't sing nor get near a guitar.

Parker talked to some TV producers who were interested in sponsoring Elvis in a Christmas special. They argued: the Colonel wanted Elvis to wear a tuxedo and sing Christmas carols, the producers wanted him to look sexy and mean in a black leather motorcycle suit and talk about his past. Elvis liked the producers' idea, but he was afraid he couldn't pull it off, that he had lost his image. He went on a new diet and his body became lean and hard; his expression intense.

When the show was videotaped, he had to walk onto a small stage, the size of a boxing ring. In the small studio audience were Elvis's friends. At the last minute Colonel Parker selected pretty women to sit up front. Scotty Moore, D.J. Fontana, and Charlie Hodge were seated on stage with their instruments. For a while Elvis sat and made fun of himself like the time in Florida when the cops made him sing without moving, the time when fans got so carried away they smashed D.J.'s drums, and the time when a girl had sneaked into his house, and Elvis said to her over the intercom, the lyric, "If you're lookin' for trouble, you've come to the right place." He talked about the popularity of the Beatles and the political songs of Bob Dylan and Joan Baez. Singing some of his old favorites, like "Blue Suede Shoes" and "Love Me," his body writhing even as he perched on his chair, he realized his strong urge to prove he was different and still as good as the current popular singers. It had been eight years since he'd gotten to sing the way he wanted to. He sang southern blues songs, like "One Night." His eyes turned sleepy, sad, and sullen as he bit his lip and sank deeper into the rhythms. By the end he knew he had squeezed something mysterious and haunting out of the songs. Inside he was happy. This music was all that mattered really.

After the show the people in the studio were jumping with excitement. Elvis looked boyishly amused. He felt gratified but tired from all the effort. The producers clapped him on the back and said, "That was terrific, the best you've done since nineteen fifty-six. Stop making movies and get back into your music."

That's right, thought Elvis. He was starved for people in the audience that he could hear and respond to. "Do you think the world is ready for a rockin' daddy?" he joked.

20: Comeback

The rave notices that the NBC-TV special received prompted Colonel Parker to start looking for a suitable place for Elvis to make a spectacular comeback live performance. Meanwhile Elvis took off for Aspen, Colorado, for a month with Priscilla and Lisa Marie before he had to work on the last movie he'd been signed up to do, *Change of Habit*. Some of the boys and their wives joined them.

One day when Elvis and Priscilla were holding Lisa Marie's hands as they took her for a walk in the snow, Priscilla said, "You know, Elvis, you've been working so hard you haven't noticed I have nothing to do."

"You have Lisa Marie." He thought of his mother and how she loved to spend as much time with him as she could when she wasn't working.

"I can't be with Lisa Marie all day. I love her, but sometimes I go crazy. She's your child too." Priscilla stopped walking and bent down to roll and pat a large ball of snow together. Elvis joined her and rolled a slightly smaller ball, which he set on top of Priscilla's. "You don't understand," she said, making a head for the snowman. "You like to play with Lisa when you're home, but you always go back to your work. I have nothing to occupy me. Being a wife and mother isn't enough." Lisa laughed and stuck a stick in the snowman's chest.

Elvis understood what she meant and wanted to make her forget her unhappiness. He said, "Well, we're here to learn how to ski."

Priscilla sighed. "I miss times like this when we're all together."

Shortly after the vacation Colonel Parker called Elvis on the phone: "M'boy, we are booked for a month in the biggest, most popular hotel in Las Vegas. It has an eighteen-hole golf course, a thousand slot machines, and a dining-hall showroom that seats two thousand. It's high class. Just right for you to make your return."

"When do we open?"

"August. Right after Barbra Streisand."

Elvis hooted. "I've been away too long and all of a sudden I'm not sure those people will like me."

"M'boy, you've done it before, you can do it again. Consider it a new beginning. We'll get Balew to design your outfits like he did for the NBC show, only this time they'll be fit for a king!"

What did he have to lose? He was nobody besides a singer. Sometimes he had yearnings to lead a more normal life, but the desire to meet the demands of all those people who wanted him to sing for them was stronger. When Priscilla heard the news, she exclaimed, "Wow! Las Vegas — where the most fabulous shows are. How perfect for you, darling!"

Elvis could hardly concentrate on his film work for worrying about the songs he would do when he returned to the stage. He desperately wanted to make a success of it. He was tired of the films but as unsure of himself as in the days when he was getting started.

He threw himself into organizing. He contacted the Jordonnaires but they were working in Memphis and couldn't leave for a whole month plus rehearsal time. He contacted the male vocalist group called the Imperials who'd made his *How Great Thou Art* album with him. They could work for him and so could the Sweet Inspirations, a group of female vocalists. He hired James Burton, a popular guitarist from Alabama, as bandleader and told him to find four other men who were tops in rock 'n' roll as backup.

The first two weeks of July, Elvis rehearsed with the band, going over a hundred songs, selecting the thirty or so that he would definitely sing, the others to be added when he felt like it. He taught the band how to follow him when he wanted to play around with a line or lyric or gesture. "I need room to improvise," he told them. "That's the only way I stay loose."

The last two weeks of July Elvis and the band went to Las Vegas to work with the International Hotel's twenty-five piece orchestra. Colonel Parker, who'd been set up in an office in the Hotel, greeted Elvis with good news. "The first week is sold out, and the rest of the month nearly so. I'll bet by the time the show starts people will have to be turned away by the hundreds."

Elvis swallowed hard when he looked at the immense showroom. It was a multi-tiered dining room with ornately carved balconies embellished with paintings, cupid figurines, and chandeliers. People would be sitting there in their fanciest dresses and tuxedos. They would be mostly older people who could afford the hotel's prices, most likely people who had known of him for years. He remembered the time in 1956 when he had come to Las Vegas for $8,500 a week and his show had to be cancelled. This time he would be getting $100,000.

The outfits being prepared for him looked splendid. They were sleek jumpsuits in red, blue, white, and black. Each was different, although all were encrusted with jewels, slit down the chest, high-collared, wide-belted, and had a detachable cape. In them he felt like Superman.

Starting to arrive were newspaper reporters

and music critics whom Colonel Parker had flown in from all over to attend Elvis's comeback for free. Also hired by Parker were pretty young women who sold his photograph and scarves with his name printed on them. Banners and flags bearing his name were posted inside and outside the building.

On the day of the opening Elvis was so tense he made his band and the orchestra go through three full dress rehearsals. He wanted no slipups of any kind. Meanwhile Priscilla waited alone in a room or went swimming in the pool with the wives of their friends. Vernon played the slot machines.

In his suite at sundown, Elvis tried to eat supper but his stomach was too jittery. He could hardly sit still for a minute. Priscilla, dressed in an elegant long white gown, was wearing the gold and diamond necklace, bracelet, and ring set that Elvis had given her. Elvis put on the black outfit that now matched the color of his dyed hair. "You look like a king," said Priscilla.

"I never felt more like a country boy," Elvis mused. "There's gotta be some Power that plucked me from nowhere and brought me here."

"Too bad I can't see you come on stage. Colonel Parker says I have to slip in to my table when the lights go out and be sure to leave before they come on at the end."

"Well, you know how he doesn't like distractions," Elvis said uncomfortably. To change the subject he said, "Hey, let's call Lisa Marie and say good night."

A little later Colonel Parker, Vernon, and four of Elvis's aides met to usher Elvis down to a backstage room. Elvis was perspiring already. His legs felt jittery. His fingers drummed his thighs as fragments from songs crowded his head. On stage a comedian was telling jokes, which Elvis couldn't listen to. The Sweet Inspirations and Imperials would perform next. There'd be an intermission. Then it would be his turn. He ran his fingers through his hair, not really hearing his friends talk. His father handed him a Pepsi. "Man, I can't get used to this," he said, shaking his head. To himself he exhorted, "Come on, Presley. You've done this hundreds of times. Just sing your best . . . God be with me."

He waited behind the curtain. When the orchestra played his cue, he closed his eyes and took a deep breath. Then he stepped on stage and headed blindly for the microphone. He opened his mouth and stood braced with his guitar, knees tensed, but before one word could come out, a roar of applause and cheers from the audience greeted him. Everyone was standing.

Elvis's face lit up in a wide grin. He glanced to his friends offstage, saying "Whadyaknow?" Then he looked back at the audience, nodded his head to the beat of the music, pursed his lips, and thought, "Well, first you better hear me out!"

When the ovation subsided, he began "Wop, bop, lop bam boom/ Tutti frutti, oh Rutti/ Tutti frutti, oh Rutti/ Got a gal named Sue/ She knows just what to do/ She rocks to the East, she rocks to the West/ But she's the gal that I love best..." He let his voice dip low for a moment and ended with a wave of his hips and arms to a high-pitched, "whoopee." After the first song he felt more relaxed. He started "I Got a Woman" teasingly. "Well," he sang slowly, "well, well, well — I said that an hour ago — well." Behind him the band lightly supported his bantering, falling in quickly when he began the song in earnest. The screams and applause encouraged him to cut loose and go as far as he wanted.

Pausing to catch his breath, he talked to the people as though they were friends. "You'll see I drink a lot of wa-wa," imitating Lisa Marie, which brought laughter. "That's because the desert air is very dry and affects my throat. I've also got some Gatorade." He held aloft the bottle. "Looks as if someone has been drinking it already." Now he felt more connected to the people. He launched into "Love Me," crying out the phrase "make me oh so lonely," which evoked screams from the audience, whose feelings were deeply touched.

Singing "Love Me Tender," he walked back

and forth across the stage, leaning down to give a quick kiss to the women who clamored to get close to him. He pulled back, laughing, when he felt his diamond ring being tugged at. Beads of sweat stung his eyes.

Striding casually across the stage he went into a medley of old hits: "Jailhouse Rock," "Don't Be Cruel," "Heartbreak Hotel," and "All Shook Up." Without pausing he gyrated into "Hound Dog." People applauded wildly everytime he accented the beat with his body.

Announcing "In the Ghetto" he added, "It's been a bestseller for me lately. Something I really needed."

His body was tiring but his elation was still high. Singing "Suspicious Minds" he closed his eyes and with his arm emphatically gestured the band to go faster. Then he threw himself into a series of karate kicks and slashes and tumbles without missing a note. The audience stood and cheered. Elvis looked at them, panting, gasping, "You're fantastic, thank you, thank you."

Lovingly, his hand trembling on the microphone, he dedicated a song to Lisa Marie: "Let Me Be There."

He blew into the microphone, mocking himself. To a woman screaming, he said "Honey, you'll get bad laryngitis that way." The audience delighted in his easy-going frankness.

He closed with a song he hoped expressed his

1969—first public appearance in nine years at the International Hotel in Las Vegas

thanks to his fans: "Can't Help Fallin' In Love With You." The applause became a steady roar as he bowed and swept off, his cape flying like the wings of a great bird. Yes, it had been quite a comeback. Backstage arms embraced him. Elvis burst into sudden tears.

A reporter queried, "Why have you waited so long to perform live again?"

Collecting himself despite the commotion, Elvis managed to say, "Movie commitments. I missed people. It was getting hard to sing to a camera all day."

The critics praised him: "There are several unbelievable things about Elvis but the most incredible is his staying power in a world where meteoric careers fade like shooting stars ... Elvis was supernatural, his own resurrection ... Elvis will have another big impact on music."

21: Elvis Plays the King

Because Elvis attracted at least one hundred thousand customers at the International Hotel, more than any other star ever had, he was signed up to return in January 1970.

When he opened again he wore a new outfit — a white buckskin Indian suit with a rope of pearls intertwined with a rope of gold tassels around his waist like a wampum belt. The suit was emblazoned with a jewelled dragon. Around his neck he wore a gold medallion. He wore six gold-and-diamond rings.

There were new songs or hits made by others to which he gave a new twist. Like "Polk Salad Annie." The band was quiet except for a low rumble of the drums. Elvis looked sternly at the audience, then at his band, back to the audience again. "Let's go down to Louisiana," he began huskily. "Some of y'all haven't been down South too much." His knee made a single rotation. "Down there we have a plant that looks sumpin' like a turnip green. Everybody calls it polk salad." He paused. "That's *polk*" — he lifted his hip — "salad" — and thrust it forward, shaking it as hard as he could. Screams filled the room.

Rocking at the Houston Astrodome

Often he made fun of himself, just as a reminder that behind the show and glitter of lights was an ordinary bumbling human being. Talking about the past, he said "I used to have such long hair, guys'd see me coming down the street and say, 'Hot dang, let's get him. He's a squirrel. He's just come outa the trees'." He mopped his brow on napkins given to him by people at the front tables. Once he blew his nose in one and gave it back. The fan put it in her purse. If the crowd wasn't responding enough he'd sing harder or do something, like unzip his jumpsuit, until he evoked mild hysteria.

Las Vegas was a complete sellout. Elvis performed even though he had a flu and cough the last two weeks of the engagement. Although offers for a concert by Elvis poured in, Parker would only consider the most super locations in the world. He booked Elvis at the Houston Astrodome for three days. Elvis was glad to return to East Texas, where he'd spent so much time in the early days of his career.

He made a new album, which Parker called "Touch of Gold" and advertised that every album would have a piece from Elvis's clothing in it. "Suspicious Minds" became his first number one hit in seven years.

When Elvis signed to return to the International Hotel in Las Vegas the third time, Parker also negotiated for a film to be made that would

With his wife, Priscilla, and daughter, Lisa Marie

be sold to television. It would be a documentary made by a prize-winning director, not a musical. It was decided neither Priscilla nor Lisa Marie would appear in the film. "Too much of a risk," Parker convinced Elvis. "If they're recognized, they could be kidnapped and held for ransom."

So Priscilla was to keep Lisa Marie out of the way in California. She complained, "With all these performances you are gone from home six months of the year."

"I can't give up performing." The truth was he liked being busy, although the strain was gnawing away at his insides. "That's the way it has to be."

"Well, I can't stay at home and wait for you all the time," she said, miffed.

Ironically, the film was to be titled *That's the Way It Is*. Elvis was filmed rehearsing with his band, wearing purple eyeshades, kidding around as usual while his friends humored him and followed his pace. Then he was filmed during a performance from the moment he shut his eyes and coaxed out his first words to the climactic end when the audience exploded in unleashed energy.

After the film Elvis moved on to Madison Square Garden in New York City. He strode on stage, striking heroic poses in jest. Singing "Hound Dog" he got down on one knee, laughed and said, "Excuse me, wrong knee," and switched to the other. He realized that all he had to do was extend an arm and wave a finger suggestively to bring down the house. It's not me they want, Elvis knew. It's bigger than me. They want the love and freedom and power that I only suggest in the songs. There was such a popular demand that a fourth performance was added to the three set shows.

Another film was made of Elvis on tour of fifty big cities. This one showed the announcer pleading with the audience to keep their seats. They didn't. Elvis sang "Bridge Over Troubled Waters" in his most sincere, tremulous manner. People quieted, some in tears. At the finale Elvis ran offstage to a waiting limousine, and the announcer boomed over the loudspeaker, "Elvis Presley has left the building."

In the car Elvis put on his dark glasses, his eyes strained from the bright glare. He gazed out the window pensively. He was tired and wondered if he had really pleased the crowd. Although he earned millions of dollars and had three thousand fan clubs around the world, he could never be sure he did as well as he might.

Back home in Memphis tension filled the air. Arguments with Priscilla. Despite his wanting to take her on vacation before his next show, they were fighting.

This afternoon he watched out the window as his father sat with Lisa Marie in a cart pulled by a pony and rode around the driveway. In the room on a couch behind him Priscilla sat with legs drawn up, her arms wrapped around them tightly. "Elvis," she repeated, "Mike Stone is my karate instructor. I took up karate because you wanted me to. If I go to his exhibitions, so what? I can't help it if the newspapers make up stories. He's a friend. What about all the woman you see?"

"I don't like reading about it — or answering other people's questions," he pouted, ignoring her attack. He felt far apart from her. When he was a boy, Lisa Marie's age, he remembered his mother and father being loyal to each other through the worst of times. Why couldn't he and Priscilla be that loyal?

She said, "He at least has time for me."

Elvis turned angrily, "You knew what my life was like before we married. You lived here. You saw. I've given you everything I could."

"Oh, I know, Elvis." Her eyes appealed for understanding. "But I want to be free to go and do what I want. I want to open a boutique. I have a friend who will make the clothes that I design."

"Okay, fine."

"Elvis," she said sharply, "I am not asking you for permission." Her tone softened. "Listen, I realize now that I can't stay hidden away forever. I can't go out in public with you. You give me all the money I need, but I get all dressed up and have no place to go."

He paced the floor, hands jammed in his pockets. "I know. It's just when I'm away I like to picture you home with Lisa. I want you both to be safe."

"I've been protected too long. I've got to be able to have interests of my own. God, Elvis, you don't know how lonely it gets without you. You have your career. You're surrounded with friends. I have nothing." At the last word her voice rose shrilly and broke into a sob. Elvis sat down next to her and put his arm around her. When her tears subsided she said, "That's why I think we'd be better off divorced."

For a long time he'd feared it would come to this. They had disputed everything before many times. Sadly he looked into her lovely face — the blue eyes, soft mouth, smooth skin, and long hair. All those years she had waited for him and now that they were a true family, she wanted to leave. God knows he understood her ambitions, but he wished she'd stay the same as she used to be, his pretty little girl to come home to. "I don't want you to go," he said gloomily.

"Elvis, if you thought for one minute things would change, I'd stay. But you'll go on performing — even in foreign countries. If we're separated, then I can lead my own life, have my own work, and it won't affect you. We can still be friends. I'll always love you." She started to cry again.

Elvis fought back his own tears. "Lisa Marie won't have a real mama and daddy. I'll miss her." He lay back on the couch, tapping his foot in agitation. He thought bitterly of all the women who fought for his attention and yet he couldn't have a normal family. The one woman he'd chosen couldn't accept his life. Nor was he willing to give anything up. He stood up. "Okay, we'll arrange it," he said, leaving the room.

He went to find Lisa Marie. While Vernon led away the pony cart, Elvis picked Lisa up and rubbed noses with her. He kissed her hair, passionately wishing he could mean to her all that his mama had meant to him. She started a fragment of a song that he'd once taught her. He squeezed her tightly.

While the divorce was being arranged, Elvis went on with his scheduled appearances, totalling 168 that year. The newspapers printed stories which made him so angry he wanted to fight anyone who made fun of him. There were also times when he seemed to have no energy. He took sleeping pills regularly in order to escape despairing thoughts. When in August, 1972, the divorce was finalized, he was glad he had his work to occupy him.

He came down with a strep throat. The doctor advised him to take a long rest, but Elvis didn't want to cancel his engagements. He knew the band members and vocalists depended on him for their jobs. He didn't want to let them down. Besides, Colonel Parker had planned a TV special called *Aloha from Hawaii,* to be beamed by satellite to forty countries, with the proceeds benefiting the KuLee Cancer Fund.

Elvis tried to be enthusiastic for the spectacular show, but he added a new song to his repertoire, "Separate Ways," into which he poured all his feelings about parting from Priscilla.

22: Decline

On his fortieth birthday, January 8, 1975, Elvis was in the Memphis Baptist Hospital, wide-awake despite the aluminum foil over the windows to help him sleep by keeping the sunlight out. He had high blood pressure — hypertension, the doctors called it and gave him medicine to calm him down. Shoot, he'd never been able to be still for more than a minute. He also had an impacted colon, which sent shooting pains through his abdomen. The doctor chided: "Too many years of junk food and irregular eating." He remembered having been in the hospital in 1973. Then it was for pneumonia. He had had such a high fever he'd almost lost consciousness. Heck, at this rate I won't live to be fifty, he thought.

He felt old, but he didn't like anyone else saying he ought to retire. He still had fans. Why, he got hundreds of get-well cards and presents. The nurses loved getting him whatever he wanted. He wanted to please them back, but he wasn't as strong as he was when he was twenty. He felt empty, as though a change was coming on, and the thought scared him. Years ago his mother had warned him against burning himself out.

He had many visitors. Even Priscilla came to see him and tell him how well her boutique was doing in California. Linda Thompson, a Memphis beauty queen he'd dated for a long time, came every day. The ones he cared about most were Lisa Marie and his dad. It pained him that Lisa Marie was so far away from him most of the time.

When Elvis got well he went back on the road to perform again, a show on the average of every three days. He bought an airplane to get him from place to place, especially California where Lisa Marie was. He named it the "Lisa Marie." He added a new song to his program. It was the song of the South, "Dixie." "Hush little baby/don't you cry" he would sing, thinking of Lisa Marie, "you know your daddy's bound to die/ all my troubles, Lord, soon be over . . ."

He won an award for being one of the Top Ten Young Americans. He also met President Nixon at the White House. Shucks, he thought, I'm just someone who likes to sing a song.

In August he had to go back to the hospital for the same problems. The doctors ran tests. Weighing 210 pounds, Elvis was about thirty pounds heavier than usual. He was given Dexedrine to suppress his appetitite. He also had a bad sinus infection. His head was stuffed. He couldn't breathe easily, coughed often, and was hoarse. The doctors suctioned mucous from his throat and gave him antihistamines. Funny, he thought, I have to take all this medicine and yet I've got a Federal law enforcement badge to fight drug abuse.

When he got out of the hospital, he stayed home until he lost weight, for he was ashamed to be seen publicly. He feared seeing ugly pictures of himself in the newspapers. He hated his reflection in the mirror because then he felt the pressure to give up singing. But the thing he wanted most was to continue to make people happy through performing. What was his future without singing or filmmaking?

He stopped paying some of his friends, like Red and Dave, to work for him. They were starting fights in public and saying bad things about him. People were pressuring him to finance their business deals. He wanted to be left alone. He felt as though his fuse was burning up. To unwind he spent hours singing spirituals by himself or with friends like J. D. Sumner. He'd close his eyes, bow his head, and hold each word tenderly on his lips. Only in singing such songs as "Lord Open My Eyes that I May See," "Sweet, Sweet Spirit," and "Rock My Soul" did he let out his feelings. "They put my mind at ease," he explained.

He got his weight down reasonably toward

the end of 1976 in time for his month at Las Vegas's International Hotel. Then he went on vacation with a young model named Ginger Alden and, tempted by good food, he gained and gained until spring when he reached 230 pounds. Now he knew how his mother felt when she struggled against her weight. It was like a hidden enemy that had to be fought constantly. He tried going on a liquid protein diet.

Suddenly in April his abdomen hurt excruciatingly. The doctor sent him to the hospital for tests and told him that his colon was twisted and should be operated on. Elvis resisted: "No, wait, I don't want any operation." Twelve days later it got better and the doctor decided it was just an intestinal flu. Tests revealed though that a liver problem was causing his ballooning weight. Puffiness in the face was one of the symptoms. But, he could go home as long as he took his medicine.

Shortly before his next tour Elvis made out his will.

Reluctantly Elvis let himself be fitted for new outfits in a much larger size. Once when he performed he split his pants and felt like a fool. Colonel Parker said, "It doesn't matter. They love you anyway." Elvis was sure he was wrong and worked even harder than before. The tour was gruelling. He found he couldn't move without getting short of breath.

Before his performance June 26th in Indianapolis, Colonel Parker encouraged him, "Don't worry, I'll handle everything. You just sing. There's nothing wrong with your voice. Your records have been hits for twenty-three years. Don't forget your eighty-three hits and sixty-five LP albums." Elvis didn't answer him.

The auditorium was like a circus, with souvenirs hawked along with cotton candy. Backstage Elvis slumped, feeling as if all his medications had taken away his energy. His friends looked as gloomy as he felt. When the band played his cue, he closed his eyes and prayed. Someone prodded him.

Elvis walked on stage under the bright lights. The applause came — hard, but not fervent. That alarmed him. He would have given anything to be off the stage, but he forced himself to go on. He sang stiffly, limply pointing his guitar at the band. He grinned, embarrassed, a shell of his former self. As he sang "Are You Lonely Tonight?" his eyes squinted in the glare. During "Teddy Bear" he dutifully handed out the initialled scarves Parker had told him to. He didn't bend over to kiss anyone. He hoped the Sweet Inspirations and the Jordonnaires were covering for him.

For the first time he felt the urge to introduce his father in the audience. The spotlight shone on Vernon, who was looking wan after having had a recent heart attack. Then he introduced Ginger, "My new fiancée," he said. As the spotlight fell on her, he joked, "Don't hog it now," to the audience's amusement.

Feeling better Elvis sang a forceful new song called "My Way." It went: "The end is near/ I face the final curtain/ my life is full/ but through it all/ I did it my way/ There were times/ I'm sure you knew/ I bit off more than I could chew/ The record shows/ I took the blows/ and did it my way..."

At the end he bowed quickly, smiled even though he knew he'd been awful, and left the stage. His friends were there to say hollowly, "It was great, just great."

"Man, I don't know. I'm operating on one cylinder." He was relieved to go back to Memphis and not have to worry about another tour until August.

Lisa Marie came for two weeks. He rented the amusement park for her one day and took her on all the roller coasters, dodgem cars, and ferris wheel as many times as she wanted. He played racquetball and swam every morning in order to lose weight faster. He was still annoyingly short of breath at times.

On the morning of August 16th around 9:30 Elvis lay awake in his circular bed while Ginger, beside him, slept. Prior to going to bed he had gone to the dentist and played a rousing racquetball match with Ginger and another couple. His chest suddenly hurt him. He got up and went to his immense red-carpeted bathroom. Before going to bed he had taken six of his pills. Now he took four more and sat down on the lounge to read.

All at once he felt dizzy, as if he were going to faint. Panicked, he thought, I've got to get help. But this mansion was not like the two-room house he'd been born in. No one would hear him. Before he knew it, he fell on the floor, his heart sputtering to a stop within a few minutes.

By the time he was discovered and the doctor brought in, he had long since stopped breathing. The doctor pounded his heart and tried to revive him. Elvis's body was taken to the emergency ward of the hospital for more attempts but it was hopeless. Elvis was dead. "Cardiac arrhythmia" was the cause, which is a difficult-to-detect heart disease that can be the result of sinus medication, appetite suppressants, and sustained emotional and physical stress.

The word went out around the world, and fans flocked to Memphis to gather in grief. An ocean of flowers was sent to Graceland. Elvis's body, dressed in a white suit with a light blue shirt and white tie, was laid in an open casket in Graceland's foyer. In three hours, ten thousand people filed past the casket, many sobbing as they looked at Elvis's still-handsome face. He was forty-two years old, having died at the same age as his mother plus two days.

On Thursday, August 18th, a funeral was held. The pallbearers were Elvis's closest friends, and only about two hundred of Elvis's friends and relatives were allowed to be present. "Sweet Sweet Spirit" closed the ceremony. Elvis's body was entombed in the family's white marble mausoleum. Later, after thieves tried to break in, Elvis's and his mother's caskets were moved and placed side by side in a meditation garden on the property of Graceland.

People would find thousands of ways to honor his spirit and remember him. For he had been a man who had imprinted himself on his time. Nothing would be the same after him for anyone anywhere in the world. He had opened up possibilities for the future of music which otherwise might have remained closed. Elvis became part of us all.

Credits

Photo credits: The photographs on pages 4, 102, 113, 116 and 157 courtesy of Wide World Photos; those on pages 8 and 102 courtesy of United Press International; on pages 10, 68 and 162 courtesy of Globe Photos. The photograph on page 75 courtesy of the author.

Lyric credits: Page 38—"I Love You Because" by Leon Payne; © Copyright 1949. Renewed 1976 by Fred Rose Music, Inc. Used by Permission. All rights reserved. Page 52—"That's All Right" copyright © 1947 by St. Louis Music Corporation. Copyright renewed. Controlled by Unichappell Music, Inc. (Rightsong Music, publisher) International copyright secured. All rights reserved. Used by permission. Pages 61-62—"Good Rockin' Tonight" by Roy Brown. Copyright © 1948—Blue Ridge Publishing Corporation, copyright renewed and controlled by Fort Knox Music Company. Used by permission. All rights reserved. Page 67—"Tryin' to Get to You" by Charles Singleton/Rosemary McCoy. Copyright Slow Dancing Music Inc., Motion Music Company. World rights assigned to and administered by Slow Dancing Music, 1978. Page 69—"Long Tall Sally" by E. Johnson and R. Penniman, Copyright © 1956 by Venice Music, Inc., 8300 Santa Monica Blvd., Hollywood, California 90669. Pages 78-79—"Baby Let's Play House" by Arthur Gunter, published by Excellorec Music Co. Page 91 "Heartbreak Hotel" words and music by Mae Boren Axton, Tommy Durden and Elvis Presley. © 1956 by Tree Publishing Co. Inc. Used by permission of the publisher. Page 155—"Tutti-Frutti" by D. La Bostrie and R. Penniman. Copyright 1955 Venice Music, Inc. 8300 Santa Monica Blvd., Hollywood, California 90669. Page 173—"My Way" words by Paul Anka, music by J. Revaux and C. Francois. Original French lyrics by Gilles Thibault. © Copyright 1967 by Societe des nouvelles editions Eddie Barclay, Paris, France. © Copyright 1969 for U.S. by Spanka Music Corporation, New York, New York. Used by permission. All rights reserved.

AUTHORS GUILD BACKINPRINT.COM EDITIONS are fiction and nonfiction works that were originally brought to the reading public by established United States publishers but have fallen out of print. The economics of traditional publishing methods force tens of thousands of works out of print each year, eventually claiming many, if not most, award-winning and one-time best-selling titles. With improvements in print-on-demand technology, authors and their estates, in cooperation with the Authors Guild, are making some of these works available again to readers in quality paperback editions. Authors Guild Backinprint.com Editions may be found at nearly all online bookstores and are also available from traditional booksellers. For further information or to purchase any Backinprint.com title please visit www.backinprint.com.

Except as noted on their copyright pages, Authors Guild Backinprint.com Editions are presented in their original form. Some authors have chosen to revise or update their works with new information. The Authors Guild is not the editor or publisher of these works and is not responsible for any of the content of these editions.

THE AUTHORS GUILD is the nation's largest society of published book authors. Since 1912 it has been the leading writers' advocate for fair compensation, effective copyright protection, and free expression. Further information is available at www.authorsguild.org.

Please direct inquiries about the Authors Guild and Backinprint.com Editions to the Authors Guild offices in New York City, or e-mail staff@backinprint.com.